# Heirs Apparent

# HEIRS APPARENT

## Solving the
## Vice Presidential Dilemma

### Vance R. Kincade, Jr.

*Praeger Series in Presidential Studies*

Westport, Connecticut
London

Library of Congress Cataloging-in-Publication Data

Kincade, Vance R. (Vance Robert)
    Heirs apparent : solving the vice presidential dilemma / Vance R. Kincade, Jr.
       p.  cm.—(Praeger series in presidential studies, ISSN 1062–0931)
    Includes bibliographical references and index.
    ISBN 0–275–96866–9 (alk. paper)
    1. Vice-Presidents—United States—History.  2. Presidents—United States—
Succession.  3. Presidents—United States—Election.  I. Title.  II. Series.
JK609.5.K56  2000
973'.09'9—dc21      99–055876

British Library Cataloguing in Publication Data is available.

Copyright © 2000 by Vance R. Kincade, Jr.

Library of Congress Catalog Card Number: 99–055876
ISBN: 0–275–96866–9
ISSN: 1062–0931

First published in 2000

Praeger Publishers, 88 Post Road West, Westport, CT 06881
An imprint of Greenwood Publishing Group, Inc.
www.praeger.com

Printed in the United States of America

The paper used in this book complies with the
Permanent Paper Standard issued by the National
Information Standards Organization (Z39.48–1984).

10  9  8  7  6  5  4  3  2  1

To my family and friends, who did not lose faith in me.

# Contents

# Introduction

The average American knows very little about this nation's vice presidents, except for those who have become president. When George Bush defeated Michael Dukakis in November 1988, he became a member of an exclusive club of incumbent vice presidents who became president. This list includes John Adams, Thomas Jefferson, and Martin Van Buren. Adams and Jefferson were elected prior to the formation of a modern party system so their elevation to the presidency was not as unique. Since the formation of the second party system in the 1820s, only Martin Van Buren and George Bush have successfully run for president while serving as vice president. This study will attempt to explain why and how Van Buren and Bush were able to achieve the seemingly impossible elevation to the presidency. This study will also make some predictions surrounding Vice President Al Gore's attempt in 2000 to join Van Buren and Bush.

The rise of Van Buren and Bush to the presidency will be carefully studied with a focus on their respective years as vice president. The vice presidency will be analyzed to answer several questions. First, what is the dilemma that faces a vice president with presidential ambitions? Was this dilemma created with the office of vice president in 1787? How has the vice presidency evolved in these two centuries under the Constitution? Have these changes helped or hindered the presidential ambitions of a vice president?

Martin Van Buren and George Bush were not the only incumbent vice presidents to run for president since Thomas Jefferson's victory in 1800. I will briefly analyze the unsuccessful campaigns of John C. Breckinridge in

1860, Richard Nixon in 1960, and Hubert Humphrey in 1968. Their defeats help to reinforce what I call the vice presidential dilemma. This dilemma is simply the difficulty of an incumbent vice president to become president. The failure of these three vice presidents also offer insights that can be useful in the ultimate explanation of the successes of Van Buren and Bush.

The body of this work will be a comparison of Van Buren and Bush. Where did these two individuals come from? How did they become vice president in the first place? What were their relationships with their predecessors? Did Van Buren and Bush owe their vice presidency and any future offices to the presidents under whom they served, Andrew Jackson and Ronald Reagan? The actions of both Jackson and Reagan to support or hinder their vice presidents' attempts to succeed them will be compared as well.

This study will also take a close look at the presidential campaigns of Van Buren in 1836 and George Bush in 1988. What similarities emerge from these two campaigns? Both candidates faced opposition from within their own party, and they both faced candidates from opposition parties that were very disorganized following the two terms of the incumbent presidents. Van Buren and Bush both made controversial decisions at the time when it came to their choices of running mates; the effects of these discussions on their campaigns need some scrutiny.

The methods of campaigning in 1988 differ dramatically from those used in the 1836 election. Both share the ultimate goal of attempting to gain public support. Van Buren's main effort to defeat his opposition in 1836, William Henry Harrison, Hugh White, and Daniel Webster, was through the extensive use of the newspaper. George Bush, in contrast, used television to assist him in his 1988 campaign against Michael Dukakis. I will place these two methods of campaigning for president under the microscope in the hope of shedding light on how the media of the times was used to gain the White House.

Following the comparison of Van Buren's and Bush's successful campaigns, I will use several models and theories espoused by political scientists to explain presidential elections. Were the elections of Van Buren and Bush following political cycles common in the United States? Were Van Buren and Bush the correct choices to fill the role of presidential leadership style that was needed in 1836 and 1988? Did they emerge as presidential candidates just prior to the waning of the political coalition that had elected their predecessors? Were Van Buren and Bush selected by the public to consolidate the achievements of their predecessors rather than to rock the boat? Finally, the use of a new model developed by political historian Allan J. Lichtman and Ken DeCell to explain presidential elections will help to show that Martin Van Buren and George Bush benefited from economic and political circumstances to win the presidency. These political and economic circumstances are referred to as "keys" by Lichtman and DeCell in their study. If a candidate has less than six keys turned against him, the presidential election is his. Van Buren and Bush emerge from their study as the rightfully elected presidents in 1836 and 1988.

This comparison study should elucidate the problems of the vice presidency and help explain the elections of Martin Van Buren and George Bush. Do visible and active vice presidents, such as Van Buren and Bush, emerge from the darkness that has shrouded other vice presidents and hindered even their mention as a possible presidential contender? In a broad sense, this study may provide a blueprint for Al Gore or for future politicians looking for another road to the White House, which has been dominated in recent years by governors and senators. Perhaps the vice presidency is not a dead-end job that many continue to believe it to be.

## WHAT IS THE VICE PRESIDENTIAL DILEMMA?

The vice presidency was not an important issue during the debates over the Constitution in Philadelphia in the summer of 1787. The Constitution that was ratified in 1789 hardly mentions the office at all. Basically the vice president would be the man finishing second in the Electoral College. He would serve as president of the Senate with the responsibility of selecting officers and breaking any ties that may result after voting. Article Two also provides the vice president's other role: "In case of the Removal of the President from Office, or of his death, resignation or inability to discharge the Powers and Duties of the said Office, the Same shall devolve on the Vice President."

From this perspective, the vice presidency appears to be a very important office. The only debate in 1789 was who would serve as vice president under George Washington. John Adams was selected by the majority of electors over eleven other candidates. John Adams as the first vice president wielded much more power than most vice presidents. In his eight years as vice president, Adams broke twenty-nine ties in the Senate. Adams did not enjoy the office or his position of being number two in the land. In describing the vice presidency to his wife Abigail, Adams explained his office's lack of importance: "My country has in its wisdom contrived for me the most insignificant office that ever the intention of man contrived or his imagination conceived."[1] Adams' opinion aside, the first vice president was able to use the office as a springboard to the presidency in 1796.

The vice presidency may have maintained the position as a stepping stone had political parties not evolved in America. The founding fathers opposed the development of parties or factions, but in the 1790s, such groups developed anyway. This development had great effects on the vice presidency. The election of 1796 resulted in the Federalist, John Adams, as president and a Republican, Thomas Jefferson, as vice president. This arrangement would be viewed as impossible from today's vantage point but was not corrected for another four years.

Adams faced Jefferson once again in his quest for reelection in 1800. Each presidental elector had two ballots to cast. Republican electors gave every one of their ballots to Jefferson and his candidate for vice president, Aaron Burr. Jefferson defeated Adams, but he had the same number of electoral votes as Burr. Following the guidelines in the Constitution, the election would be decided in the House of Representatives, which was controlled by lame duck Federalists. Rumors of political bargains and intrigue involving Aaron Burr circulated wildly. Jefferson finally was elected on the thirty-sixth ballot, but he never trusted his vice president again. An amendment to the Constitution was necessary with the advent of conflicting political ideologies and political parties. The Twelfth Amendment to the Constitution, ratified in 1804, solved the problem of the 1800 election by requiring presidential electors to vote separately for president and vice president. This amendment answered the political problems of the day, but it also severely damaged the importance of the vice presidency. The vice presidency was no longer a reward for being the second most popular candidate. It became a political prize for loyal party politicians. The stepping stone to the presidency shifted to the office of secretary of state for the next twenty years.

With the exception of Martin Van Buren and George Bush, no incumbent vice president since has become president except through the death or resignation of the president. Becoming the president through demise of the president had its complications at first. Debate began immediately in 1841, with the death of President William Henry Harrison, about whether Vice President John Tyler was the president or just acting president. This issue was not solved definitively until the ratification of the Twentieth Amendment to the Constitution in 1967. The Constitution now states that the vice president will become president if something, such as death, resignation, or disability, happens to the president.

The powers of the vice president have not recovered from the ratification of the Twelfth Amendment in 1804. Following the ratification, vice presidents were usually older, experienced politicians from important states such as New York. Vice Presidents George Clinton and Elbridge Gerry had been distinguished politicians, but their careers were long over when they were selected to fill the number two spot. Both Gerry and Clinton served well, but their advanced ages brought health problems and ultimately death prior to completing their terms in office. As the United States was facing conflict in the 1840s and 1850s and moving toward civil war, vice presidents were selected to bring sectional balance to presidential tickets. The vice-presidential candidates' political views were not of great concern, unless, of course, they became president after the death of the incumbent president. Consider John Tyler and Millard Fillmore, who became president following the deaths of Presidents William Henry Harrison and Zachary Taylor. Both faced hostile attacks from within their own party and they were subsequently abandoned by the very people who had positioned them in the vice presidency.

Beginning with Abraham Lincoln's reelection campaign in 1864 and continuing through the Gilded Age, vice presidents were chosen to balance and to unify different wings of political parties. The vice presidents of this period were not distinguished politicians, and they often disappeared into oblivion following their terms in office. The accidental presidents of this period, Andrew Johnson and Chester A. Arthur, had difficult presidencies and were not nominated to serve a term of their own. The first accidental president to receive his party's nomination for his own term was Theodore Roosevelt in 1904.

Roosevelt was selected much the same way as vice presidents were in the nineteenth century, but he was not viewed as an obscure politician; rather, he was seen as a political threat to Republican bosses in New York. Roosevelt was young and becoming too powerful in New York. The powerless office of vice president was perfect to rid New York bosses of this menace. Unfortunately, President William McKinley was dead within a year, and the hated Rough Rider took the reins of government and forever weakened the power of the bosses.

A contemporary of Roosevelt's was a political scientist from Princeton with strong views on government. Little did he know that he would become president himself one day. Woodrow Wilson believed that the vice presidency was a very weak office: "His position is one of anomalous insignificance and curious uncertainty."[2] Wilson followed his beliefs about the vice presidency when he became president in 1913. Vice President Thomas Marshall was left out of all decision making during his eight years as vice president under Wilson. Marshall was nowhere to be seen when Wilson was in Europe negotiating at Versailles and was in the dark during the period when Wilson was recovering from his stroke. The president's wife refused to give Marshall access to her convalescing husband. Marshall kept his humor when he discussed his position: "Once there were two brothers, one ran away to sea, the other was elected vice president, and neither of them was heard of again."[3]

Following World War II, the vice presidency has gained in importance and stature. The vice presidency was given a permanent seat on the National Security Council and its incumbent often represents the president in ceremonial functions around the world. In recent campaigns, vice presidents have been selected for their loyalty to the presidential candidate and, as in the past, for their ability in some instances to bring important states into the ticket's grasp. The vice president remains second on the totem pole and must assume whatever role the president creates for him, large or small. An active politician who becomes vice president must control his impulses and stand behind the president, right or wrong. This position may seriously disrupt and possibly destroy any chance for effective leadership in the future, as was the case with Hubert Humphrey's support of Lyndon Johnson and the war in Vietnam.

The prestige and importance of the vice presidency created by the founding fathers has clearly not recovered from the Twelfth Amendment. The role of the vice president since 1804 fluctuates with each administration. Many politicians viewed the job in the nineteenth and twentieth centuries as a dead-end job with no opportunity for advancement. Daniel Webster declined the vice-presidential nomination in 1848 by saying, "I do not propose to be buried until I am really dead."[4] Ironically, had Webster accepted the Whig nomination he would have achieved his lifelong wish of becoming president upon the death of Zachary Taylor in 1850. This negative impression of the vice presidency continued into this century. John Nance Garner, Franklin Roosevelt's first vice president, described the vice presidency as not being worth a "warm pitcher of spit" or worse. The office has never resumed its place as a stepping stone to the presidency. Many potential voters view the vice president as lacking the independent vision or character that they want in their presidents.

All of these problems make up the vice-presidential dilemma. How can a sitting vice president be elected president when in most instances their political futures are linked to the sitting president? The dilemma of acquiring a separate sphere of influence remains. Many may question studying Martin Van Buren and George Bush because over a century separates them, but since the Twelfth Amendment was ratified in 1804, these two are the only vice presidents to solve the dilemma. Their quests for the presidency share many similarities and their stories should be told. However they achieved their goal, both Van Buren and Bush were able to become president from a position in the government that has effectively blocked candidates since the founding of this country.

## THE THREE THAT FAILED

From the time of Martin Van Buren's victory in 1836 to the election of George Bush in 1988, three other incumbent vice presidents attempted to become president. Each of these candidates failed, but they were all involved in some of this nation's most exciting elections. John C. Breckinridge battled Abraham Lincoln and two others for the presidency in 1860. Richard Nixon fought John Kennedy for the right to succeed President Dwight D. Eisenhower in 1960. Hubert Humphrey completes this list with his candidacy in the violent 1968 campaign. Each of these vice presidents lost close elections and briefly telling their stories will assist in explaining where Van Buren and Bush made the right decisions that prevented them from suffering the same fate.

John C. Breckinridge fits the mold described earlier for a vice president. Coming from Kentucky, he was nominated in 1856 to be the running mate of James Buchanan of Pennsylvania. Breckinridge assisted Buchanan's election in several ways. First, Breckinridge came from a border and slave state. Second, he had supported Stephen Douglas at the Democratic National Convention held in Cincinnati in 1856. Nominating Breckinridge to serve with Buchanan would restore harmony to the embattled wings of the Democratic party. Finally, at the age of only thirty-five, Breckinridge was a political rising star. His youth and enthusiasm struck a good balance with an elder statesman such as James Buchanan.

Breckinridge was the primary campaigner for the Democratic cause in 1856. Going on speaking tours was still not really accepted as common, but Breckinridge displayed his energetic style throughout the country. He delivered speeches in the critical states of the Mid-Atlantic and Midwest. The future vice president was well received in Illinois, Indiana, Michigan, Ohio, and Pennsylvania. Breckinridge was successful in bringing the party together behind Buchanan in 1856, and the future appeared bright for the young man from Kentucky.

Almost immediately following Buchanan's victory, the focus began to turn to the election of 1860 with Breckinridge as a prominent candidate. Many newspapers in the Northwest started discussing Breckinridge's chances in 1860 before Buchanan had been sworn in. Buchanan had expressed his desire very early not to run for a second term, so if Breckinridge could survive his term as vice president and remain on good terms with the many factions of the Democratic party, then the nomination could be his in 1860.

Breckinridge spent his years as vice president ignored by President Buchanan for much of the time. Breckinridge served as vice president in much the same way that every vice president since Van Buren has. Breckinridge presided over the Senate and was not consulted by President Buchanan on any issues. He was well respected by his Senate colleagues but virtually ignored by the administration. He confided to his friends that throughout his vice presidency his opinions were not asked for by the president on the important events of the day. Breckinridge actively opposed the wishes of Buchanan by campaigning for Stephen Douglas in his 1858 senatorial campaign against Abraham Lincoln. Buchanan wanted Douglas defeated because he opposed the Lecompton Constitution, which the president believed would end the problems in Kansas. Breckinridge followed his own convictions and aided Douglas in his narrow victory over Abraham Lincoln.

The Democratic National Convention was scheduled to meet in Charleston, South Carolina, in 1860. Breckinridge had no real organization, and he demanded that his name not be placed in nomination until other candidates from his home state had failed to seize the nomination. Breckinridge was still only thirty-nine in 1860 and his closest friends counseled him to wait for 1864, 1868, or 1872 to run for president. The convention failed to nominate a candidate because of fierce arguments regarding a slavery plank in the platform. Several delegations from the South walked out of the convention in protest. Two Democratic conventions met in Baltimore six weeks later hoping to unify behind a candidate. The main convention nominated Stephen Douglas to carry the party's banner. The rump convention, composed mostly of the delegations who walked out at the previous convention nominated Breckinridge without his permission. Breckinridge reluctantly accepted the nomination when efforts to hold a new convention failed. The Democrats were forced to run two candidates against Abraham Lincoln, the Republican nominee.

Breckinridge campaigned very little except for two speeches in Kentucky. He had to endure efforts of the president to get him and Douglas to withdraw for party unity. Efforts at fusion with Douglas supporters in some states failed, and in November 1860, Breckinridge suffered his first political defeat. He finished third in popular votes and second in the Electoral College. Even so, he was the only candidate to gain votes in all three sections of the country.

Breckinridge's campaign displayed how difficult it was to be vice president during a period when the duties were not clear. Vice presidents had to support the policies of the administration publicly or face obstacles from the rank and file of the party. Breckinridge was in a position where he could not openly discuss his views. The vice presidency was not the right place for Breckinridge to launch a presidential campaign. His political allies in Kentucky realized his dilemma and elected him to the Senate almost a year before his term was to expire. Breckinridge had tried his best to distance himself from Buchanan, but for many, he was still part of the administration. His support of Douglas in 1858 helped in some Democratic areas, but Breckinridge could not separate himself from the depression of the late 1850s and the divisions over slavery fanned by the Dred Scott decision, Bloody Kansas, and John Brown's raid. Breckinridge in the end became the defender, whether he liked it or not, of the Buchanan administration.

Other than a brief effort by John Garner in 1940 to gain the Democratic nomination, no sitting vice president ran for the top prize until Richard Nixon in 1960. Nixon's years as vice president are comparable to those of Martin Van Buren and George Bush. He served as second in command to one of this nation's most popular leaders, Dwight David Eisenhower. Nixon's early political career was one success after another. Like Breckinridge, Nixon's first political defeat occurred when he ran for president in 1960. Until that November, the political star of Richard Nixon was constantly ascending. Nixon had profited from his anti-Communist stance and his success in the Alger Hiss case to become nationally known by 1952.

With the help of former Republican standard bearer Thomas Dewey, Nixon was nominated for vice president and by clinging to the coattails of General Eisenhower, he became vice president by the time he turned forty.

President Eisenhower was determined to treat his vice president differently than his predecessors. Eisenhower did not like Harry Truman, and he believed that President Franklin Roosevelt had left him uninformed and ignorant during the war, which he felt was extremely dangerous. Eisenhower promised that Nixon would be kept informed and involved in the policies of his administration. Nixon attended all major meetings and was kept appraised of policy, but all decisions for the next eight years were made by the president. Nixon spent much of his vice presidency doing the political dirty work for Eisenhower and the Republican party. He did an admirable job while Eisenhower was recovering from his heart attack in 1955. Even with this successful first term, however, there were efforts to dump him from the ticket in 1956. Eisenhower discussed this issue with Nixon and offered him a cabinet position to give him administrative experience. In their discussions, Eisenhower also raised the Van Buren factor, explaining that no sitting vice president since Van Buren had won the presidency. Nixon wished to remain vice president, though, and was reelected easily along with Eisenhower in 1956. Nixon spent his second term traveling around the world and making a name for himself internationally. He gained public support at home after an attack on him took place during a goodwill tour to Venezuela in 1958 and by showing his toughness in his successful Kitchen Debate with Nikita Khruschev in 1959. By his actions, Nixon elevated himself into the likely Republican nominee in 1960.

Yet Eisenhower was not impressed with any of his potential successors. He finally sided with Nixon because he considered the vice president to be better than Nelson Rockefeller, the governor of New York, and John Kennedy. Eisenhower stayed out of the campaign in its initial stages and even damaged Nixon's prospects during a press conference in August 1960. When asked by a reporter about whether Nixon had any ideas that he had adopted, Eisenhower replied, "If you give me a week, I might think of one. I don't remember."[5] This statement was damaging to Nixon, but it was generally the truth. Nixon was simply Eisenhower's vice president, he did not make decisions because the nature of the office was not conducive to decision-making. Eisenhower privately reiterated his opinion that Nixon should have accepted a cabinet position offered in 1955 to give him the decision-making experience that he lacked.

Nixon campaigned as hard as any candidate in history. He had the continuous problem of defending the Eisenhower administration as well as explaining where he would take America if elected. This constant defense of the Eisenhower administration handcuffed Nixon to a degree. He owed his position to Eisenhower and could not promote programs in conflict with him. Nixon had been a political star since the Hiss case, but now he could only point to the fact that he had served with one of the nation's greatest men for the past eight years.

Nixon attempted to show his independence from Eisenhower, however, by the way he operated his campaign. Nixon organized his campaign with his own staff, refusing to include any Eisenhower men. Nixon might defend Eisenhower's policies, but it was his campaign to win or lose, and he would run his race without the political managers who helped Eisenhower to two landslide victories. Nixon wanted to be the focal point of the campaign. He would suffer the consequences for any mistakes made, but he would be the sole beneficiary of any correct decisions. Nixon and his campaign made mistakes, and Eisenhower offered to stump the country for him, but Nixon refused. This decision stunned the eager president. Nixon had been advised, however, by Maimie Eisenhower and by the president's doctors that Eisenhower should not be placed under the stress of campaigning. Eisenhower did go on one late campaign swing for Nixon, but he was unable to capitalize on the personal popularity of the man he served loyally for eight years.

Nixon was defeated by John Kennedy in 1960 in one of the closest races in history. Nixon had enjoyed tremendous success in politics in the past. During his eight years with Eisenhower, he became the most visible and possibly the most successful vice president of the twentieth century. Yet Richard Nixon was unable to balance running for president and serving as vice president as Martin Van Buren had. Van Buren would remain the last successful sitting vice president for the next thirty years and this factor would haunt one more presidential contender.

The next sitting vice president to attempt to become president was Hubert Humphrey in 1968. His campaign shares many similarities with Breckinridge's effort in 1860. Both Humphrey and Breckinridge suffered by running for president when the incumbent president was very unpopular. Breckinridge could break with Buchanan since he owed him nothing, but Hubert Humphrey owed his selection as vice president and his political position to Lyndon Johnson. Johnson may have been unpopular in 1968, but he still wielded immense power in the Democratic party, and Humphrey could not afford a premature rupture.

Hubert Humphrey would have continued his successful career in the Senate had it not been for the tragic events in Dallas on November 22, 1963. He had lost the Democratic nomination to Kennedy in 1960 and his path to the White House appeared blocked by the foreseeable future. Kennedy's assassination opened new doors to Humphrey. Following Kennedy's funeral, Humphrey met with his political advisors. "You fellows are my closest advisors," he said, "I want to become president and the only way I can is to become vice president."[6] Humphrey had been friends with Lyndon Johnson in the Senate prior to Johnson's election as vice president in 1960.

Humphrey was well aware that Johnson had already suffered a heart attack and probably would not serve in the White House for two full terms. Lyndon Johnson made the vice presidency appear to be an important job as he went through his selection process prior to the 1964 Democratic Convention in Atlantic City. The public, still grief stricken over Kennedy's death, placed a great deal of importance on Johnson's selection of a running mate. Johnson used this heightened importance by repeatedly explaining that he would select the best man qualified to serve with him and perhaps succeed him. Johnson blocked efforts to put Robert Kennedy on the ticket and finally selected the popular senator from Minnesota. Humphrey toured the country with Johnson during the campaign and rode with LBJ to a landslide victory over Republican Barry Goldwater in November.

Humphrey became vice president for a man who demanded absolute loyalty and did not want anyone stealing the limelight from him. Humphrey had a limited role as vice president, with responsibility for getting Johnson's legislation through the Senate. Humphrey's positions were overlooked by Johnson when it came to foreign policy, particularly concerning America's role in Vietnam. Johnson even held National Security Council meetings without informing his vice president. Humphrey was trapped and out of the loop in his role as vice president. His role in the administration was what Johnson decided it would be. After a couple of years as vice president, Humphrey had no constituency except for LBJ. Johnson also became annoyed when he believed Humphrey was receiving too much media coverage. The president even told Humphrey to continue to be a loyal vice president and not be concerned with how the media portrayed him. Humphrey probably would have run for reelection with Johnson but Johnson notified him that he would not seek another term. Johnson told Humphrey of his decision just one day before he announced it to the country. Humphrey was stunned by Johnson's decision and uncertain of his future path. Johnson told Humphrey, "If you're going to run, you'd better get ready damn quick."[7] Humphrey decided to run for president, but not to enter any of the presidential primaries. Johnson's efforts in encouraging negotiations with Vietnam helped Humphrey's campaign in April and May 1968. Humphrey effectively used this period to secure enough delegates to win the nomination.

Humphrey's favorable position changed with the death of Robert Kennedy in June. Financial supporters who despised Kennedy stopped contributing to Humphrey's campaign after the assassination. Humphrey also had renewed fears that President Johnson might still decide to run and be drafted at the convention in Chicago. Humphrey stopped campaigning for two weeks. He was at a crossroads. He was dominated by Johnson on one side and by the left wing of the party on the other, who wanted someone to carry Kennedy's banner and defeat Richard Nixon. Humphrey consulted his advisors on his next move. He was advised by some to break with

Johnson over Vietnam. Others suggested that he should resign the vice presidency at the convention to show his independence. Humphrey eventually chose to reject all of this advice at this time.

The Democratic convention in Chicago was a disaster for Humphrey. From his perspective, he failed to separate himself from the president, and he allowed Johnson supporters to write the Vietnam plank in the platform. Humphrey trailed Richard Nixon by fifteen points in the polls and led George Wallace by only seven points following the convention. Humphrey finally decided, at this point, to break with Johnson. In a speech on September 31, 1968, Humphrey spoke without the vice presidential emblem, and he explained his position on Vietnam. Humphrey's break with Johnson revived his campaign with large contributions and also brought the anger of President Johnson who refused to campaign for Humphrey throughout October.

Humphrey continued to gain on Nixon during October, and when Johnson announced peace talks in Vietnam on Halloween, victory was within sight. Even the president came around and finally endorsed Humphrey in a campaign spectacular in the Houston Astrodome just prior to the election. Another week might have brought victory, but Humphrey, like Nixon and Breckinridge before, failed to win at the polls. Van Buren's accomplishment was safe for another twenty years.

Of the three vice presidents who failed, Humphrey discussed the vice presidency and the problems of running for president the most. He explained a year later what went wrong in his campaign:

After four years as Vice President . . . I had lost some of my personal identity and personal forcefulness. . . . It would have been better that I stood my ground and remembered that I was fighting for the highest office in the land, I ought not to have let a man who was going to be a former president dictate my future.[8]

In his memoirs, Humphrey discussed the vice presidency in detail. He understood the limited role of the vice president. "A Vice President cannot sustain a dissenting position. He can express his views freely if discreetly, but on matter of high policy, once his views have been heard and rejected, he must accommodate to the limited scope of his role."[9] In dealing with the president, Humphrey offered two choices: "I am convinced that a Vice President, regardless of talent and the President's personality, has a choice between two relationships, acquiescence and hostility. The Vice President simply cannot move without the President's seal of approval."[10] Finally, Humphrey directly discussed the benefits and difficulties of a sitting vice president running for president:

When a sitting Vice President becomes a candidate for President, as I did, all these things become important. While I have a very special feeling and sometime affection for the office, its possibilities, even the frustrations, in 1968 the Vice Presidency was both an asset and liability—an asset in terms of preconvention political power and a liability when it came to free-wheeling, self assertive politics.[11]

The three candidates discussed shared the problem of losing one's identity. How does one remain a political power when one occupies an office without any real power? The vice presidency has become an office with only one purpose, that of taking over after a president dies. Presidents do not like to be reminded of their mortality and often brush aside and ignore their vice presidents. Even if a vice president is ignored, he must support the policies of the administration. A failure to support the administration would end all hope a vice president has in winning an election on his own. Breckinridge, Nixon, and Humphrey were all excellent politicians, but for each, the vice presidency was a road block that they could not overcome. Their failures help to reinforce how remarkable the victories of Martin Van Buren and George Bush were. How were they able to overcome the road block that stopped the others?

# 1

# Becoming Vice President

Martin Van Buren and George Bush followed different paths on their way to the number two position in the land. Van Buren and Bush come from completely different backgrounds. Van Buren was the product of a middle-class innkeeper's family. Bush was raised in the wealthy eastern establishment of the 1920s. They were both reared with a sense of the importance of education, and they took advantage of every opportunity available to them, including the opening of doors by their families and friends.

Van Buren attached himself to important individuals in New York. Many of these patrons shared Van Buren's Dutch ancestry, and they were active in politics early in the nineteenth century, when the first party system in America was born. Bush became a war hero in World War II while he was in his early twenties and, after graduating from Yale University, started an oil company in Texas. His father, Prescott Bush, was a U.S. senator, and he helped to stir a political interest in his second son George. The young Bush did not enjoy the initial political success of Van Buren, but, like him, he was able to gain the support and interest of leading politicians. Bush earned the patronage of Richard Nixon and then Gerald Ford.

Van Buren and Bush acquired influence in national and state politics, and they ultimately found themselves involved in presidential politics. Van Buren in 1824 and Bush in 1976 both supported political adversaries of the men under which they would eventually serve as vice president. Van Buren did not believe that Andrew Jackson was qualified to be president in 1824, and Bush was considered as a possible running mate for Gerald Ford in 1976 and was, thus, a political opponent of Ronald Reagan.

The attitude of Van Buren toward Jackson and of Bush toward Reagan changed rather quickly. Van Buren became an active supporter of Andrew Jackson by 1826 and was instrumental in his election to the presidency in 1828. Jackson reciprocated the hard work by appointing Van Buren as his secretary of state, the commonly accepted stepping stone to the presidency since the ratification of the Twelfth Amendment in 1804. Internal conflict within the Jackson administration surrounding the wife of the secretary of war and the mistrust of Vice President John C. Calhoun led to Van Buren's resignation and ultimately his nomination for vice president in 1832. Jackson believed that Van Buren had been wrongly denied the position of minister to England by Calhoun, so he replaced Calhoun with Van Buren.

Bush actively sought the Republican nomination in 1980 against Ronald Reagan and won a stunning victory in the Iowa caucuses. Bush, however, failed to follow up in New Hampshire with the knockout blow. Reagan recovered momentum and moved on to gain the nomination easily. Bush finished a distant second and was seemingly out of the picture. During the Republican convention, however, circumstances were such that George Bush became Ronald Reagan's running mate. Negotiations failed to get Gerald Ford on the ticket, so Reagan decided on Bush, everyone's second choice.

This section focuses on Van Buren's and Bush's roads to the vice presidency and seeks to answer the following questions: How important was the attachment of Van Buren and Bush to leading politicians in preparing them for their role as vice president? Did Van Buren and Bush constantly have to battle their family backgrounds to become capable politicians on their own? Did their early opposition to Andrew Jackson and Ronald Reagan hurt their relationship with the respective future presidents? Finally, what did Van Buren and Bush bring to the 1832, 1980, and 1984 campaigns that benefited the top of the ticket? Each answer is important to understand how the vice presidency became a means to an end for both Van Buren and Bush.

At any time during their paths to the vice presidency, Van Buren and Bush could have found themselves out of politics altogether. There was a possibility that Van Buren could have been appointed to the Supreme Court long before he became vice president. Bush might have remained head of the Central Intelligence Agency. He enjoyed his tenure at the CIA and was given credit from both parties for reforming the agency's image. Had Gerald Ford been reelected or had President Carter accepted Bush's offer to stay out of politics and remain at the CIA, the vice presidency may have never happened for Bush. Becoming vice president was not preordained for either man. In Van Buren's case, many had doubts several months before the nomination. Bush's nomination was seen as virtually impossible only hours before he received the call. Looking at how these two became vice president is a necessity in learning how they both became president.

## THE MAGICIAN LEARNS HIS TRICKS

Becoming vice president was not necessarily in the cards when Van Buren was born. He did not come from a wealthy family or from one that had made its name in politics. Van Buren did not fight in the Revolutionary War, and his generation would be a new breed to serve in national office. Before becoming vice president, all previous occupants of the office either enjoyed long political careers from respected families or had served in America's armed services. Van Buren's rise to the vice presidency does seem to have some magical connotations to it.

Martin Van Buren was born on December 5, 1782, in Kinderhook, New York. He was the third of five children born to Abraham and Maria Van Buren, both of whom were of Dutch descent. His father was a local inn-keeper, and the Van Burens decided that Martin should be trained to become a lawyer. After attending the village school until the age of fourteen, Martin became a clerk for the respected Francis Sylvester, Esq. Following a loan from a fellow of Dutch descent, John P. Van Ness, proving that he was not born with a silver spoon in his mouth, Van Buren was sent to the New York office of the distinguished lawyer and politician William P. Van Ness, John's brother. Van Ness acted as Van Buren's benefactor and life-long supporter. Van Buren thrived in New York and was licensed in November 1803 as an attorney of the Supreme Court, then returned home to Kinderhook to practice law with his half brother.

While in Kinderhook, he met and married Hannah Hoes on February 21, 1807. During their twelve-year marriage, Hannah gave Martin four sons. Hannah's death in 1819 ended a terrible three-year period in Van Buren's life. Both of Van Buren's parents had died in the previous two years. Van Buren never remarried, and the focus of the rest of his life was on his sons and politics.

Van Buren had been exposed to politics by his father, who opposed the Federalists and was an early supporter of Thomas Jefferson around the turn of the century. Van Buren shared his father's convictions and was subsequently attacked by many Federalists in the region. Through the efforts of William P. Van Ness, Van Buren became a representative to a Republican convention of Columbia and Rensselaer counties to nominate a candidate for the New York House of Representatives. Van Buren was only eighteen at the time of this appointment. At the convention, he was an able assistant to the veteran politicians and received their help in his future endeavors.

The young Van Buren decided to run for elective office in 1812. Following a successful career as a lawyer, he ran for the state senate. He faced opposition from remnants of the Federalist party and from those who wanted the Bank of the United States to be rechartered. President Jefferson opposed the Bank of the United States created by Alexander Hamilton and wanted the bank charter to expire. Van Buren campaigned hard against the bank and won a narrow victory.

Once in the state senate, Van Buren's attention immediately turned to presidential politics. In 1812, he found himself supporting New York City's popular mayor Dewitt Clinton for president. Van Buren would be a political enemy of Clinton's for almost twenty years, but not in 1812. This time Van Buren acquiesed to the majority in the State Assembly and supported Clinton's presidential aspirations against the reelection of President James Madison. The issue of 1812 was war with Great Britain. Van Buren wanted the war to be brought to a quick and successful conclusion. Clinton's campaign ended in failure, but Van Buren continued to grow politically in stature and influence. Van Buren's position on the war was well founded, and the struggle was brought to a relatively quick if not successful conclusion. The War of 1812 also destroyed the Federalist party once and for all in New York. Following the presidential election, Van Buren fought for candidates in opposition to Clinton. In 1813, Van Buren supported the reelection of Governor Daniel Tompkins in a direct battle with Clintonians. Van Buren's organization succeeded in getting Tompkins reelected, and he was reelected himself in 1816. While in the state senate, Van Buren was a great supporter of internal improvements, especially a canal for New York. Van Buren continued his rise in New York politics by gaining appointment as New York's attorney general from 1815 to 1819. This position was finally taken away from him when Dewitt Clinton and his followers returned to power.

Some observers thought that Van Buren's political career was over when his second term in the state senate ended in 1820. They were wrong. Van Buren's opposition to Clinton helped to rally similar men behind him. Van Buren and his allies, known first as the Bucktails and eventually the Albany Regency, gained control of New York politics for a generation. Van Buren's political organization was unable to prevent Clinton's reelection as governor, but the Bucktails did gain control of both houses of New York's legislature. The New York state senate rewarded Van Buren with his appointment to the U.S. senate in 1821.

Van Buren left New York in the capable hands of the Albany Regency and moved to the national stage. Here, Van Buren saw the opportunity to become directly involved in presidential politics and in the formation of a new political party. Van Buren traveled throughout the South visiting politicians and espousing the principles of Thomas Jefferson in the hopes of reinvigorating political party competition. He argued that "parties are not only inevitable but fundamentally a good thing for the public interest when properly harnessed."[1] During this period in Washington, the so-called Era of Good Feelings, President James Monroe practiced a policy of amalgamation in the hopes of eliminating partisan squabbles. Monroe shared the founding fathers' fear of factions and hoped to eliminate political parties.

His virtual unanimous reelection in 1820 seemed to show that his policy was working. Van Buren did not share Monroe's opinion and he hoped to build a new party behind the popular secretary of the treasury, William Crawford from Georgia.

Crawford, like Van Buren, shared the Jeffersonian principles of limited government. Van Buren decided to direct the Georgian's campaign. Van Buren saw no need to adopt a new process to nominate Crawford for the presidency. He decided to use the congressional caucus system that had previously nominated both Madison and Monroe. This decision was one of the few mistakes of Van Buren's political career. The public was beginning to question how democratic the caucus system was. Only about a third of congressional Republicans attended the caucus that selected Crawford in 1823, so the treasury secretary's victory was not all that important. Crawford had also suffered a severe stroke and was virtually bedridden for months. Van Buren continued to run Crawford's campaign for president in 1824, and he tried to garner former President Jefferson's endorsement when he visited him at Monticello. Jefferson contributed his thoughts on the campaign, but he did not come out publicly for Crawford.

Van Buren was also waging a battle to retain control of the New York legislature, which would award New York's electoral votes. He was, however, unable to secure for Crawford a majority of New York's electoral votes. The candidates in 1824 included John Quincy Adams, Henry Clay, and Andrew Jackson, who all had supporters in New York. When the legislature finished its balloting, twenty-five votes went to Adams, seven votes to both Crawford and Clay, and none to Jackson. Jackson may have done poorly in New York, but following election day, he had a plurality (though not a majority) of electoral and popular votes. Under the Constitution, the election would be decided in the House of Representatives, since no candidate had a majority. Van Buren still hoped that he could secure victory for Crawford in the House.

The members of the House could only select the president from three who had the most votes nationally—Adams, Jackson, and Crawford. Henry Clay finished fourth and was out of the contest, but his position as Speaker of the House made him very powerful. Each state would have one vote to cast based on which candidate received the most votes in a state's delegation. Van Buren hoped to keep the election deadlocked until he could swing enough states to bring Crawford victory. Van Buren believed that New York's delegation was deadlocked, and that split would prevent John Quincy Adams from getting a majority of the states. New York Congressman Stephen Van Rensselaer was besieged by Adams supporters warning him of the consequences of a prolonged House fight. Van Rensselaer failed to consult with Van Buren and, following what he believed was guidance from above, voted for Adams, giving him New York's vote and the presidency.

Van Buren's first effort in presidential politics had ended in failure, but he was determined to learn from his mistakes and achieve victory in 1828. Van Buren did not blame Henry Clay for Adams' election. He gave no credence to the corrupt bargain charges that haunted the Adams administration: Some critics charged that in return for being appointed secretary of state, Clay threw his support behind Adams and made him president. Van Buren simply dedicated himself to educating the country to oppose the beliefs of John Quincy Adams and to finding a person around whom to create a political party. The runner-up in the 1824 election intrigued Van Buren. Van Buren, like most Americans of the time, respected Andrew Jackson for his military exploits, and he came to the conclusion that Jackson was the man to support.

Van Buren sought support for the old general by setting up alliances among leading politicians and newspaper men. Van Buren sealed one alliance with the editor of the *Richmond Enquirer*, Thomas Ritchie. He told Ritchie that he believed a new future party would consist of "the planters of the South and the plain Republicans of the North." Van Buren also became acquainted with Jackson's strongest supporter in Tennessee, John Overton, leader of the Nashville Junto, a similar organization to Van Buren's Albany Regency. Van Buren used his mouthpiece in New York, the *Albany Argus*, to maintain his political control while he went on a much celebrated trip to the South to form a party behind Jackson. He met with William Crawford and Thomas Jefferson and sealed an important alliance with Adams' vice president, John C. Calhoun. Vice President Calhoun used his considerable political influence to help Jackson in 1828 and, in four years, was Jackson's heir apparent. Calhoun was on the ticket of both Adams and Jackson in 1824 and had no closeness with Adams.

Van Buren had to withstand attacks regarding his political activities. The Adams administration was attempting to follow the policy of James Monroe by trying to eliminate the need for political parties and unify the country. Van Buren disagreed and spoke out against Adams' efforts to bring Henry Clay's American System into operation. Clay's system consisted of a national bank, a protective tariff, and congressionally financed internal improvements to unify the country.

Van Buren met with President Adams in May 1827, and the president had this impression of the man running his opponent's campaign:

He is now acting over the part in the Union, which Aaron Burr performed in 1799. Van Buren, however, has improved in the act of electioneering, upon Burr, as the State of New York has grown in relative importance in the Union. Van Buren has now every prospect of success in his present movement, and he will avoid the rock on which Burr afterwords split.[2]

Van Buren and like-minded senators vehemently opposed a proposal by Adams and Clay to send representatives to a conference of American countries in Panama. Van Buren's arguments against the Panama Conference were printed in the *Argus* as well as articles by the paper's staff defending Van Buren from attacks from opponents hoping to defeat his reelection bid to the Senate in 1827:

No greater proof can be desired of the fitness of the president incumbent, than the increasing virulence and implacable animosity with which he is assailed by Federalists. They appear to regard him as the heart of the political body with which he is connected, and conceive that if a successful blow can be aimed at him, it would consumate the destruction of the party of which he is a member.[3]

Van Buren continued his efforts for Jackson and his standing battle with Dewitt Clinton. Clinton could make Van Buren's reelection difficult, and he could potentially cause problems for Jackson in New York. Clinton was a friend of Jackson's, and there were rumors that he would run with Jackson in 1828. These rumors concerned Calhoun and could have ruined his agreement with Van Buren before the election.

Clinton's sudden death in February 1828 worked to Van Buren's advantage. He gave an impassioned eulogy for his long-time adversary and resumed his efforts to shore up his support in New York. Van Buren advised Jackson not to speak publicly on any issues, especially the tariff bill being debated in Congress at the time. Van Buren favored the bill with some changes but hoped that the bill would not affect Jackson's support in the South and the West.

Upon his reelection to the Senate in 1827, Van Buren spent the next year securing New York's electoral votes for Jackson. Van Buren did not want a repeat of the events of 1824. He was attacked by Adams' newspapers for controlling New York's electoral votes. The *Argus* came to his defense on its own on September 18, 1828:

We are conscious that we owe an apology to our readers for having said so much upon this subject, and particularly for having spoken thus freely of Mr. Van Buren. It is not our habit to do so. It is rare that we allude to that gentleman, and never except in the vindication of him from the assaults of his adversaries. We are not his eulogists. His fame requires nothing of that sort at our hands.[4]

Van Buren was convinced by his advisors that the best way to guarantee Jackson's success in New York was for Van Buren to run for governor. Van Buren, the master politician, in his acceptance speech for the nomination for governor, made no mention of how this could aid him in achieving his main objective, making Andrew Jackson president:

Deeply sensible that I owe whatever of public consideration I may possess, to the favour of the Republicans of New York, and conscious of my inability to discharge the debt of gratitude that rests upon me. I have made it the rule of my conduct not to decline any station to which it may be their pleasure to call me.[5]

Van Buren's supporters campaigned hard in his race for governor. When election day arrived on November 4, 1828, the *Albany Argus* let its feelings be known: "And Let the Cry Be, Jackson, Van Buren and Liberty."[6] Both Jackson and Van Buren won comfortably in New York and Jackson easily defeated John Quincy Adams for the presidency.

Almost immediately following the election, rumors spread regarding Van Buren's future. Was he destined to serve as New York's governor for the next four years or was his destiny elsewhere? Some argued that Van Buren's future should be at the side of General Jackson. This debate persisted throughout the winter of 1828–1829. Less than a month after the election, the *Argus* printed reports for opposition papers, such as the *National Intelligencer*, describing the competition for succeeding Jackson that had already begun. The *Argus* printed "that already a rivalry has commenced between Mr. Van Buren and Mr. Calhoun for the next presidency."[7] This rumor had no basis at this time. Van Buren was still governor of New York and had not been offered a cabinet post. Van Buren congratulated the people of New York for electing Jackson in his address to the State of New York early in 1829:

A result which while it infuses fresh vigour into our political system and adds new beauties to the Republican character, once more refutes the odious imputation that Republics are ungrateful; dissipates the vain hope that our citizens can be influenced by aught save appeals to their understanding and love of country, and finally, exhibits in bold relief, the omnipotence of public opinion, and the futility of all attempts to overawe it by denunciations of power, or to seduce it by the allurements of patronage.[8]

During his brief tenure as governor, Van Buren worked on reforming New York's banking system. In early March, just prior to Jackson's inaugural, it became public knowledge that Van Buren would be nominated to become secretary of state. The *Argus* printed with pride its approval of this selection of New York's governor for this cabinet post:

While in the Senate of the United States, he was confessed on all hands to be the ablest debater in that body. His abilities are equally conspicuous as a writer. Bred to the bar, where he has risen to the highest eminence, he is familiar with the principles of law, both domestic and national. With the interests and sentiments of the great state of New York, which is an empire within itself, he is equally familiar. He is her favorite son, and she is entitled to be represented by such a son in the cabinet of the nation. With polished manners, great address, sound discretion, legal and political skill and wisdom, Mr. Van Buren is the very man who ought to have been selected to manage the diplomatic intercourse and foreign relations of the country.[9]

The *Argus* failed to mention that the position of secretary of state was considered to be a stepping stone to the presidency. The appointment was even more important considering that Jackson was not in the best of health and was expected to serve only one term.

Van Buren explained in his autobiography that he did not seek the position of secretary of the state: "This position like every other office or nomination save one, bestowed upon me in the course of my long public life, came to me without interference on my part, direct or indirect, and in the execution of the well understood wish of the great majority of the political party of which I was a member."[10] Van Buren was easily confirmed by the Senate, and he resigned his position as governor on March 12, 1829, after serving three months. The *Argus* reported a Philadelphia newspaper's satisfaction with Van Buren's selection as the new secretary of state. "Had ambition alone governed him, he might well have decided rather to be first in New York, then second at Washington. The president himself must have peculiar satisfaction in having at his right hand the first man of the greatest state in the union, and who enjoys at the same time so large a share of the esteem of all his fellow citizens."[11]

During his little more than two years as secretary of state, Van Buren did not accomplish much. He did get France to agree finally on a settlement of debts or spoliation claims remaining from the War of 1812. Van Buren had a much greater impact on domestic issues. He was instrumental in getting President Jackson to veto the Maysville Road Bill in 1830. Van Buren convinced Jackson that the bill was unconstitutional because this federally funded internal improvement would be built solely in one state. Jackson followed his secretary's advice and vetoed the measure. The fact that the road to be constructed was located in Henry Clay's home state of Kentucky was an added incentive for Jackson's veto. Jackson still viewed Clay as being involved in the Corrupt Bargain of 1824, and he blamed Clay for allowing newspapers to publish allegations against his wife during the recent campaign. Jackson's wife died shortly after the election, and Jackson attributed her death to these reports.

Van Buren spent his time as secretary of the state gaining the friendship of the president. He had known Jackson when they both served in the Senate in the early 1820s, but a friendship grew during their frequent horseback rides around Washington. Van Buren's primary activity during his tenure at the State Department consisted of attempting to maintain harmony and alleviate tensions within Jackson's cabinet.

Former President John Quincy Adams had this impression of Van Buren in the summer of 1829:

Mr. Van Buren is now Secretary of State. He is the manager by whom the present administration has been brought into power. He has played over again the game of Aaron Burr in 1800, with the addition of political inconsistency, in transfering his allegiance from Crawford to Jackson. He sold the State of New York to them both. The first bargain failed by the result of the choice of the electors in the legislatures. The second was barely accomplished by the system of party management established in that state; and Van Buren is now enjoying his reward.[12]

The primary concern of the cabinet was the marriage of Secretary of War John Eaton to Margaret Timberlake. The controversy over this marriage became known as the Eaton Affair. Eaton had met Margaret while he was residing at her father's boarding house. Margaret's first husband believed that Eaton had stronger personal feelings for his wife than were appropriate. Before Timberlake could follow up on these charges, he was sent back to sea where he met his untimely death. Eaton professed his love for Margaret and asked his close friend Andrew Jackson for advice following Jackson's victory in 1828.

Jackson had known Margaret since she was a little girl. He advised Eaton to marry her quickly and prevent rumors of an affair prior to Timberlake's death from being levied against them. At this time, Jackson was mourning his own wife's death, the cause of which he blamed on such charges. Jackson had run away with his future wife Rachel years before and married her before her divorce was final. Technically, Rachel was a bigamist, and this charge was printed in opposition newspapers during the campaign. Eaton followed Jackson's advice and married in January 1829 with Jackson present. The issue closed, Jackson nominated Eaton as secretary of war, and they all moved to Washington.

The practice in Washington at the time was for each cabinet member to host dinner parties. This practice was disrupted by members of Jackson's administration who were friendly to Vice President Calhoun. The vice president's wife was a product of southern society, and she refused to entertain the former barmaid Peggy Eaton. Other Cabinet wives followed Mrs. Calhoun's example. President Jackson was furious and, after vouching for Peggy's virtue, ordered his Cabinet members to entertain the Eatons. The only Cabinet member who treated the Eatons with kindness was Martin Van Buren. The secretary of state had been a widower for years and was not concerned about the propriety of entertaining a former barmaid. Van Buren later discussed this period in his autobiography:

After looking at the matter in every aspect in which I thought it deserved to be considered I decided, for reasons not now necessary to assign, to make no distinctions in my demeanor towards, or in my inter course with the families of the gentlemen when the President had, with the approbation of the Senate, selected as my

Cabinet associates, but to treat all with respect and kindness and not to allow myself by my own acts, to be mixed up in such a quarrel.[13]

Van Buren's treatment of the Eatons endeared him to the president and brought uneasiness from Calhoun. Problems with the Eatons and the Cabinet continued and eventually destroyed Jackson's group of advisers, setting into motion questions over succession between Van Buren and Calhoun. Van Buren did not want any of this behind-the-scenes activity to be printed by his mouthpiece in New York, and the *Argus* followed his wishes. "We know well Mr. Van Buren's sentiments on this subject," it wrote, "from the first indications of a disposition to agitate the public mind as to General Jackson's successor, he has deprecated that course, not only as uncalled for and unnecessary, but as one which could not be otherwise than injurious to the public welfare."[14]

The vice president believed that Van Buren was intriguing against him. At about the same time, William Crawford returned to the spotlight and discussed an issue with the president that had angered Jackson for over a decade. Crawford informed Jackson that in 1818 Calhoun, in his position as secretary of war, recommended that Jackson should be punished for his actions in Florida. Jackson had seized Spanish forts while fighting the Seminole Indians and then executed two British subjects without approval from Washington. Jackson's activities almost brought the nation to war. Jackson had been under the impression that Calhoun had supported his actions. Calhoun had never said anything publicly or to Jackson to alter this impression. Jackson finally wrote to Calhoun requesting an explanation. Jackson received instead a fifty-page letter from Calhoun defending himself. Jackson was furious with his vice president. For his part, Van Buren knew about Calhoun's actions in 1818 prior to Jackson's election, but he denied any involvement in this controversy in his autobiography: "I instantly decided to have nothing to do with the affair and decided to express my opinion upon the question he submitted to me."[15]

Van Buren was concerned with rumors that he was plotting to become president in 1832 and that he was the source of all the problems in the Jackson administration. While on one of their rides together, Van Buren suggested a solution to Jackson's problems. He would resign from the Cabinet. This action would allow Jackson the opportunity to request that the rest of his Cabinet do the same. The Eatons could be sent out of Washington, and Jackson could start all over again with a new Cabinet. Jackson was initially opposed to this plan but finally accepted Van Buren's resignation.

Van Buren submitted his resignation to Jackson on April 11, 1831. The text of the resignation was printed two weeks later. Before the resignation became known, the *Argus* once again defended Van Buren from charges regarding succession: "His whole political career gives the lie to such a charge. There is not a man in the United States who has labored more constantly and we may add more successfully to consolidate and preserve entirely the great Republican party throughout the Union, than Martin Van Buren."[16]

The correspondence between Jackson and Van Buren regarding his resignation has survived. It displays the concern Jackson had for his now former Cabinet member. Van Buren hoped that his resignation would end any speculations regarding him and succession:

From the moment of taking my seat in your cabinet, it has been my anxious wish and zealous endeavour, to prevent a premature agitation of the question of your Succession; and at all events to discountenance, and if possible, repress the disposition at any early day manifested, to connect my name with the disturbing topic.[17]

Jackson responded the following day, indicating a desire to return Van Buren to the government as soon as possible. "I cannot, however, allow the separation to take place without expressing the hope that this retirement from public affairs is but temporary," he wrote, "and that if any other station the Government should have occasion for services that value of which has been so sensibly felt by me, your consent will not be wanting."[18]

Van Buren left Washington and returned to his home in New York, still the topic of rumors. By the middle of May 1831, the story surfaced that Van Buren was to be sent by Jackson to England to become the new American minister. The *Argus* questioned whether sending Van Buren out of the country would end personal attacks against him. "Will placing the Ocean between him and the presidential chair remove the jealousies of our contemporary?—or will he persist in biting at the 'Magician' across the great waters?"[19]

Throughout the summer, Van Buren made preparations for his departure to England. News stories describing Van Buren selling his furniture and returning his horse did not stop rumors about the vice presidency. The *Argus* reprinted these rumors during the summer and denied their accuracy regarding Van Buren becoming Jackson's running mate in 1832. Opposition papers questioned the proposed convention of Jackson supporters scheduled for May 1832 as a possible forum to nominate Van Buren for the vice presidency. The *Argus* printed reports from other newspapers regarding Van Buren: "*The American Sentinel* of Philadelphia, repeats the assertion of the *U.S. Telegraph*, that the object of the proposed republican national convention is the nomination of Mr. Van Buren for the Vice Presidency."[20]

Van Buren discussed Jackson's desire to send him to England and the issue of succession in his autobiography:

In this connection the English Mission was spoken of as probably the best means of carrying out his wishes if he should persist in them, and either then or subsequently I brought to his notice my understanding of the acceptance of that appointment as a virtual abandonment of any expectation or hope my friends might otherwise entertain on the subject of my accession to the Presidency.[21]

The *Argus* continued to deny rumors, and it stated after Van Buren's departure on August 12, 1831, "Mr. Van Buren is not and will not be a candidate for the vice presidency."[22] These denials aside, the political enemies of Van Buren, Daniel Webster, Henry Clay, and John C. Calhoun, still believed that he would be Jackson's running mate. This triumvirate plotted while Congress was out of session to mortally wound Van Buren's political career. The three men concluded that they should defeat Van Buren's nomination as minister to England. Van Buren was sent to England by Jackson, but his nomination needed the approval of the Senate. Any ties in the Senate would be settled by Vice President Calhoun when Congress reconvened.

In London, Van Buren won the affection and approval of the British government. He was aware of the political rumblings at home, but he did not allow them to distract him from his duties. When Congress reconvened late in the fall of 1831, Jackson wrote to Van Buren about the possibility of becoming his running mate. Jackson was concerned whether the Senate would confirm Van Buren:

If I am reelected, and you are not called to the vice presidency, I wish you to return to this country in two years from now, if it comports with your views and your wishes. I think your presence here about that time will be necessary. The opposition would if they durst try to reject your nomination as a minister, but they dare not, they begin to know if they did, that the people in mass would take you up and elect you vice president without a nomination; was it not for this, it is said Clay, Calhoun and Co. would try it.[23]

Throughout December 1831, the *Argus* constantly printed stories about the possible rejection of Van Buren in the Senate and then the likelihood that Van Buren would become vice president. According to Van Buren, he had no thoughts on becoming vice president and was embarrassed that it was being discussed. The *Argus* declared: "It is not in accordance with Mr. Van Buren's wishes, or with those of the great mass of his friends in this state, that his name is thus urged before the public; nor is he a candidate for a place, for which a sincere partiality in some instances and questionable professions of friendship in others, may have named him."[24]

The debate in the Senate gave Clay, Webster, and Calhoun the opportunity to vent their anger toward Van Buren and his nomination. Senator Thomas Hart Benton of Missouri paid close attention to the debate and wrote about it in his memoirs. Benton believed that Van Buren was viewed

as a roadblock to the presidential aspirations of Clay, Webster, and Calhoun. In his memoirs, he offered four reasons why the triumvirate contin-
ually worked for rejection of Van Buren's nomination:

1. The instructions drawn up and signed by Mr. Van Buren as Secretary of State,
   under the direction of the President, and furnished to Mr. McLane, for his guidelines in endeavouring to reopen the negotiations for the West Indian trade.
2. Making a breach of friendship between the First and Second offices of the government—President Jackson and Vice President Calhoun, for the purpose of
   thwarting the latter, and helping himself to the Presidency.
3. Breaking up the cabinet for the same purpose.
4. Introducing the system of "proscription" [preventing people from being in the
   cabinet] for the same purpose.[25]

The attackers in the Senate had an advantage because Van Buren could
not defend himself. Van Buren was even accused of being against Jackson's
veto of the Maysville Road Bill. In the end, the enemies of Van Buren
organized the voting in the Senate so that it ended in a tie and allowed
Vice President Calhoun to cast the deciding vote. Calhoun voted against
Van Buren and believed that he had killed Van Buren's political career.
Unfortunately for Calhoun, his assessment was wrong.

Van Buren's political allies consoled and counseled him on what his next
move should be. His friend New York Congressman Churchill C. Cam-
breleng wrote immediately after the rejection to Van Buren: "Come back
as quick as you can—we have no triumphal arches as in ancient Rome,
but we'll give you as warm a reception as every Conqueror had."[26] Cam-
breleng changed his thoughts on the following day January 28, 1832. "My
plan is that you should not arrive till about the time of or rather a week
or two after the meeting of the Baltimore Convention."[27]

Thomas Hart Benton went into greater detail regarding the vice presidency and what Van Buren should do in his letter to Van Buren also dated
January 28, 1832:

The vice presidency is the only thing, and if a place in the Senate can be coupled
with the trial for that, then a place in the Senate might be desirable. The Baltimore
Convention will meet in the month of May, and I presume it will be in the discretion
of your immediate friends in New York and your leading friends here, to have you
nominated; and in all that affair I think you ought to be passive.[28]

The anger over Van Buren's rejection was obviously great in New York.
In February 1832, Republican members of the New York legislature wrote
to President Jackson to express their concern:

The State of New York,—sir, is capable in itself, of avenging the indignity thus offered to its character in the person of its favorite son. But we should be unmindful of our duty, if we failed in the expression of our sympathy with your Excellency's feelings of mortification, at this degradation of this country you love so well.[29]

The president replied ten days later, praising Van Buren and denying the charges made against him:

I owe it to the late Secretary of State, to myself and to the American people on this occasion to state, that as far as is known to me, we had no participation whatever in the occurrences relative to myself and the second officer of the government, or in the dissolution of the late cabinet; and that there is no ground for imputing to him having desired those removals from office, which, in the discharge of my constitutional functions, it was deemed proper to make. During his continuance in the cabinet, his exertions were directed to produce harmony among its members; and he uniformly endeavored to sustain his colleagues. His final resignation was a sacrifice of official station to what he deemed the best interests of the country.[30]

In a note sent to Van Buren at about the same time, Jackson made clear his desire to avenge his defeated minister and make him vice president. "The people will properly resent the insult offered to the Executive, and the wound inflicted in our national character, and the injury intended to our foreign relations, in your rejection, by placing you in the chair of the very man whose casting voted rejected you."[31]

Back in the United States, discussion focused on making Van Buren vice president to take advantage of the situation and help him eventually become president. William Lewis, a Van Buren supporter and politician, discussed this view with another Van Buren ally, A. C. Flagg, in a letter written in February:

From all quarters heard from, the people manifest a determination to run him for the Vice Presidency, and upon this, I think, they are resolved. I am sure, if it is desired, or even expected to make Mr. Van Buren President, this occasion to place him prominently before the nation should be promptly embraced. If the party cannot now, under existing circumstances, succeed in electing him Vice President, he can never hope to be President.[32]

The *Argus* quickly jumped on the bandwagon in support of Van Buren in March 1832:

If the Republicans of the Union desire to place the name of Mr. Van Buren before the nation as a candidate for Vice President, New York will cordially unite with them, and will give him her electoral votes in a manner that will exhibit to the world her estimate of him, she has delighted to honor.[33]

Finally on March 14, 1832, in a note to his long-time friend and New York colleague William Marcy, Van Buren decided to allow his name to be offered as a vice-presidential candidate. "If the Republicans of the United States think my elevation to the Vice Presidency the most effectual mode of testifying to the world their sentiments with respect to the act of the President and the vote of the Senate, I can see no justifiable ground for declining to yield to their wishes."[34]

Van Buren's name was placed before the national convention of Jackson supporters in Baltimore in early May, and he received the nomination on the first ballot. The rumors of Van Buren running with Jackson for the past two years had finally proven true. Van Buren viewed his nomination in his autobiography as the spontaneous demand of the people:

I was made a candidate for the office of Vice President of the United States in the pursuance of the spontaneous and united demand of the democracy of the Nation; a complimentary vote was given in Convention to two other gentlemen by the delegates of their respective states, who were, in point of fact, as friendly to my selection as were those who advocated it from the first, but the nomination was forthwith made unanimous in form as it was in the wishes of the mass of the democratic party.[35]

Van Buren ran a very quiet campaign for vice president. First of all, he did not return to the United States until July. For the rest of the summer and fall he remained at home to escape a cholera epidemic. The campaign of 1832 was clearly a choice between Andrew Jackson and Henry Clay and did not revolve about their respective running mates. Van Buren was attacked on several issues. Questions again arose over his attitude toward the Maysville Road veto. Clay supporters raised Van Buren's supposed hostility to the War of 1812. Most attacks on Van Buren centered on the belief that he was riding the coattails of Andrew Jackson to the vice presidency and ultimately the presidency.

The attacks of Clay supporters did no good. Jackson won reelection in November easily. Shortly after the results were known, Jackson offered his congratulations to his new vice president. "Your triumph is complete and the faction in the Senate condemned by an overwhelming majority of the people."[36] The *Argus* also offered its congratulations to Van Buren in December 1832:

The public will, justly characterized by Mr. Van Buren, as the true spring head of Democratic Principles, has decreed, that on the fourth of March next, the man whom John C. Calhoun sought by casting vote, to destroy, shall occupy the high and honorable station, which the Carolina nullifier has proved himself unworthy to hold.[37]

When the electoral votes were counted in February 1833, the final results were as follows: Jackson 219, Van Buren 189, Clay 49, and Sargent 49. Upon his notification of being elected vice president, Van Buren offered these words, reprinted by the *Argus*, following the inauguration. "I cannot refrain from seizing this occasion to express my deep and grateful sense of honor conferred upon me by my fellow citizens, and my determination that exertions shall be spared to render myself worthy of the generous confidence they have reposed in me."[38] Martin Van Buren had become the eighth vice president of the United States. He was just one step away from the presidency. Andrew Jackson was not a well man and he was, according to observers, looking feeble at the inaugural. There were rumors that Jackson planned on resigning in a year or two, handing over the presidency to Van Buren, his heir apparent.

How was Van Buren able to come so far so fast? He benefited politically from serving under a man who took offenses, no matter how minor, personally, especially if it was criticism of his military exploits. John C. Calhoun had every right to question the actions of Jackson in Florida in 1818. Van Buren had a good idea of Calhoun's actions prior to Jackson's election in 1828, but he dismissed them as unimportant. Jackson's break with Calhoun was not inevitable, and Van Buren would not have been Jackson's running mate had it not been for the incident more than a decade earlier. Jackson executed two British subjects while attacking the Seminoles in Florida.

Probably the most fortunate factor in Van Buren's relationship with Andrew Jackson and his rise to the vice presidency was that he was a widower as was Jackson. This situation enabled Van Buren to spend a lot of time with Jackson on horseback rides discussing the issues of the day and personal concerns. Being a widower also helped Van Buren to stay out of the Eaton Affair. Van Buren did not have a wife, or hostess, who could object to entertaining Mrs. Eaton. Even Jackson had to deal with his own niece's refusal to entertain the Eatons. Van Buren was able to sit back and watch Calhoun destroy his chances to succeed Jackson without having to lift a finger. By the spring of 1833, Martin Van Buren had made himself through hard political work the heir apparent to Andrew Jackson. He would have to be careful during his term as vice president or he might suffer the same fate as Calhoun. Van Buren needed to maintain the support of Jackson and to convince others that he was the man to follow the old general.

Van Buren had come a long way from the tavern in Kinderhook. He had been successful in finding people to help him rise politically. Van Buren was able to use people for political purposes but not gain their hatred. His elevation to the vice presidency was indeed magical. His skill as a politician has been compared by his biographer Holmes Alexander to that of France's great politician Talleyrand in the book *The American Talleyrand*. Both men were survivors and masterful manipulators of men and events.

## EVERYONE'S SECOND CHOICE

George Bush's rise to the vice presidency was more plausible than that of Martin Van Buren. Bush had family background and considerable wealth. Politics was a natural outlet for one in Bush's position. Being wealthy and a resident of Texas, Bush became a contender for vice presidency several times in his political career. He was a possible candidate in 1972, 1974, and 1976. It finally took a run for the White House in 1980 for Bush to earn a place on the national ticket. Bush was a credible candidate that needed someone to select him as their first choice and not remain everyone's second choice.

George Herbert Walker Bush was born June 12, 1924, in Milton, Massachusetts, the son of Prescott and Dorothy Bush. Very early in George's life, the family moved to Greenwich, Connecticut. Bush's father was an investment banker and would later be a U.S. senator from Connecticut. Bush's mother came from the respected Walker family, their name being synonymous with the amateur golf championship between America and Great Britain known as the Walker Cup. George received the best education his parents could provide, and he graduated from the exclusive Philipps Andover Academy in 1942. George was expected to enter Yale University, but World War II intervened, and he enlisted instead in the navy in June 1942. He began his life away from home in the Pacific.

Bush earned his pilot wings at eighteen and was said to be the youngest commissioned pilot in the navy at that time. He was a carrier pilot during the war against Japan. He won three Air Medals and the Distinguished Flying Cross for heroism and extraordinary achievement after his plane was shot down, and he was rescued off the Bonin Islands. The rest of Bush's crew perished in the crash. The film footage of Bush's rescue survived and was used throughout his political career. Bush was discharged in 1945 and married Barbara Pierce of Rye, New York.

George finally did attend Yale University, where he was captain of the baseball team and graduated Phi Beta Kappa, earning his degree in economics in just two and a half years. He could have followed in his father's footsteps and become an investment broker, but he wanted to strike out on his own in the oil business in Texas. In 1948, George moved his family, which included three sons and daughter, to Odessa, Texas. He learned about the oil business, from drilling to processing, with friends from Yale. With the help of his uncle and father, Bush started his own oil company, Zapata Petroleum Corporation in 1951. The company was a success, and Zapata Off Shore Company was created to exploit the potential of offshore drilling and made George Bush a very wealthy man.

While Bush was building his company in Texas, he became involved in politics. His father's position as a U.S. senator did not impede this process. Texas was predominantly Democratic, but Bush lived in a Republican stronghold in the Houston suburbs. He started his political career in 1964, supporting Barry Goldwater for president. Bush decided to run for the Senate against the Democratic incumbent Ralph Yarborough. Bush campaigned under the Goldwater banner and espoused conservative positions. He lost the race to Yarborough 56 to 44 percent, but he still did better than expected in Lyndon Johnson's Democratic state. Bush was very proud of his showing in 1964. "We ran ahead of Goldwater by 200,000 votes and polled more votes than any Republican had ever won in the states' history," he said, "that gained me some national recognition."[39]

Bush's defeat did not deter him from continuing in politics. As part of a lawsuit, he was able to get his congressional district in the Houston suburbs redrawn, and the new district elected him to Congress in 1966 and reelected him in 1968. Bush was popular in the House of Representatives. Congressman John Hammerschmidt (R-Arkansas) commented, "I don't think I've ever heard a member of Congress from either party say anything adverse about George Bush."[40] Bush voted as a conservative on most issues in Congress. He supported the war in Vietnam and defended the oil business through his assignment on the House Ways and Means Committee. He did face opposition at home when he voted for the Civil Rights Act of 1968, which included an open housing provision. He survived the immediate hostility over his vote and was reelected in 1968. The new president, Richard Nixon, liked Bush, and he hoped to gain more Republican Senate seats in 1970. Nixon persuaded Bush to have another go at the Senate in that year.

Bush was expecting a rematch in 1970 with Senator Ralph Yarborough. Surprisingly, Yarborough lost the Democratic primary to a conservative protégé of John Connally, Lloyd Bentsen. Bush and Bentsen shared many similar positions on the important issues. Bush appeared to be leading in the polls as he ran his campaign without mentioning the unpopular president or vice president in his speeches. Bush gained the support of Yarborough followers who hated Connally until the final weeks of the campaign. In the final month, both Nixon and Spiro Agnew campaigned in Texas for Bush and stirred up Democratic animosity. High turnouts in Democratic strongholds turned the election to Bentsen 53 to 47 percent. Bush found himself out of the House of Representatives in January 1971 and looking for a new job.

Bush visited President Nixon and basically asked him for the job as U.N. ambassador. Nixon had grown to like Bush, and he had urged him to make his fateful Senate race in the first place. Nixon approved of Bush's request and made him ambassador for the next two years. According to his biographers, Bush enjoyed his work at the United Nations; it gave him a chance to learn diplomacy. Bush probably would have preferred to remain at the United Nations throughout Nixon's presidency, but the president had other ideas.

Following his landslide victory in 1972, Nixon began to shuffle his Cabinet and other offices. Many Nixon men took new jobs. Early in December 1972, the *Washington Post* printed rumors that Bush would join the Pentagon. Bush's future was not in the Pentagon, however, but as chairman of the Republican National Committee (RNC). The *Washington Post* wrote about the dismissal of Nixon's previous three chairmen and questioned why Bush was replacing Robert Dole.

Rowland Evans and Robert Novak discussed this new assignment for Bush in their column on December 15, 1972: They talked to GOP insiders who viewed Bush as being more loyal to Nixon than Dole. "George won't go to the bathroom without asking the White House," they wrote.[41] They concluded that Bush might not be excited about taking this new position: "This prospect can scarcely be appetizing to Bush, who would be a possibility for President in 1976 had he won his 1970 Texas race for the Senate. He would have preferred a Cabinet post, but Mr. Nixon and his Cabinet makers preferred faceless businessmen to politicians in filling vacancies."[42]

Bush became chairman of the RNC on January 19, 1973, and he promised to remain neutral in any squabbles within the Republican party. "I do not intend to be some kind of ideological spokesman for all Republicans. It is our party that believes in federalism and it is our party that must welcome diversity."[43] Bush believed that his time as chairman would be spent trying to rebuild a party that had suffered while Nixon was winning his victory in 1972. Bush learned in 1973 that his job was also to protect the party from the increasing problems associated with Watergate. Initially, Bush expected Nixon to be an active campaigner in 1974. "The President will play an active role in 1974 helping candidates," he said. "He wants to see other Republicans elected, he wants to see the party stronger. Events control so much but we have a chance. If the big issues are going our way, we could really turn things around."[44] Watergate continued to worsen; consequently, Bush did not want Nixon's help in 1974.

By September 1973, President Nixon's popularity was at 38 percent and falling. Bush had been chairman of the party for eight months and was judged with mixed results in a column by Lou Cannon of the *Washington Post*:

Bush's problem as chairman is that he's out so much speaking he doesn't really run the shop, says one knowledgeable GOP official. No one could have done a better job than he did on handling the public relations problems of Watergate. But he doesn't know the problems of campaign management, so he doesn't know what's not being done. There is no executive director to run the place, when he's away and no long range plan. So people swerve from project to project short term.[45]

Bush continued to travel and make speeches trying to separate the Republican party from the Watergate disaster. He remained loyal to Nixon almost to the very end. On August 7, 1974, Bush sent a letter to Nixon asking him to resign for his own sake as well as the country's: "If you do leave office history will properly record your achievements with a lasting respect."[46] Nixon resigned the presidency two days later, and Gerald Ford became president. Ford knew Bush while they were in the House of Representatives, and immediately Bush became involved in the debate over who would be selected as Ford's vice president.

Bush was on everyone's short list for vice president, and he was the best organized in seeking the position. Within a week following Nixon's resignation, Evans and Novak believed that Bush's prospects were growing. "As the new President was sworn in, Rockefeller had become a considerably less likely prospect than either Senator Howard Baker of Tennessee or George Bush, the gregarious patrician and transplanted Texan who heads the Republican National Committee."[47] The Bush balloon suddenly exploded when allegations were made of illegal contributions from the Nixon political machine to help Bush in his 1970 Senate race. Bush denied the allegations, but this rumor of a Nixon slush fund continued to haunt Bush later when he ran for president in 1980. President Ford passed over Bush and appointed Nelson Rockefeller as his vice president.

Bush did not remain at the Republican National Committee for long. In early September 1974, Ford asked him to become the U.S. representative in Peking. Bush had no special knowledge about China other than dealing with the Chinese at the United Nations, but he accepted the post and left the Republican National Committee after more than two years of service. His tenure with the RNC and his ability to make friends with county chairmen and learn politics from the grass roots helped Bush tremendously when he ran for president.

Although Bush had no formal training as a diplomat, his aides regarded his time in China as productive. Bush fought for American interests, and the Chinese seemed to like him. His stay in Peking was cut short, however, by President Ford. In November 1975, the president requested that Bush return home and take over the leadership of the Central Intelligence Agency (CIA). Bush did not want to leave China, but he intended to serve in any way possible for Gerald Ford. Bush commented that his stay in China was "exceptionally pleasant and hopefully productive. In a job like this, it is a little egotistical to suggest any accomplishments have been mine. There has been nothing earth shattering, but we have had some good contacts. I accept the Chinese judgment that our relationship is in reasonably good shape."[48]

Bush had little experience in intelligence work, and his appointment by President Ford raised many eyebrows in Washington. The CIA had been under attack for operations under the Nixon administration, and Ford hoped that Bush would clean up the agency's image. Bush's confirmation would not be easy because of his past service running the Republican party.

The *Washington Post* wrote after his appointment in November 1975: "In Washington, he is known as a gregarious Republican Party Loyalist. His credentials in the intelligence community are few, but his knack for getting along with people and his wide political contacts could be an asset in an agency subject to persistent criticism on Capitol Hill."[49] Columnist Lawrence Stern in the *Washington Post* wrote about the CIA and the replacement of William Colby. He expressed the belief that CIA members were not happy with Bush as their new chief. "High ranking agency insiders are skeptical about the ability of Colby's successor, no matter how quick a study he is, to testify convincingly on such issues as whether covert operations should be abolished or what sort of congressional oversight arrangements should be provided."[50]

In the Senate, Bush faced opposition because of his past political involvement. Bush promised at his confirmation hearing that he would keep politics out of the agency and that he just wanted to serve his country. Bush's nomination was not sealed until after President Ford promised the Senate that Bush would not be his running mate in 1976. With this promise from Ford, Bush was confirmed 64–27 by the Senate. Bush continued his hard work, and he did help to restore the confidence and morale at the CIA. Bush kept his promise to keep politics out of the agency and following President Ford's defeat to Jimmy Carter in November 1976, many believed that Bush might continue on as CIA chief.

Bush announced suddenly on November 25, 1976, that he would resign when Jimmy Carter took office in January 1977. Bush received praise from Democrats and Republicans alike. In a column by Evans and Novak a couple of days following his announcement, they explained what happened to make Bush resign so quickly after Jimmy Carter won the election:

Since holdover CIA directors were retained in the 1960 and 1968 transitions, there had been speculation that Bush would stay for the six months—perhaps longer if he hit it off with Carter. That was ruled out in Plains Nov. 19. "Jimmy just wasn't impressed with Bush," a key Carterlite told us. At one point, when Bush volunteered that the President-elect would probably prefer his own man at CIA, an unsmiling Carter replied coolly that was indeed the case and a new director would be ready Jan. 21.[51]

Bush left Washington in January 1977 with no immediate plans. According to his supporters, he had almost become vice president on three occasions. The first opportunity was when Bush was running for the Senate in 1970. Had he won, Bush was rumored as Nixon's running mate in 1972. The second opportunity was after Vice President Agnew resigned in 1973. Bush was a possibility for the vice presidency until Nixon selected Gerald Ford. The third opportunity was after Nixon's resignation.

Bush traveled across the country throughout 1977 and 1978, meeting with Republican leaders. At the end of this trip he decided that his future was not in Texas politics but in national politics. George Bush did not want to be someone's second choice again. He intended to run for the presidency in 1980. The road was not easy, but his experience with local Republican politics would help in running for the Republican nomination. His résumé was impressive, but Bush still had to battle for the nomination with men who had far more name recognition and charisma, such as Ronald Reagan and John Connally.

Bush was well received by local leaders throughout his travels in 1978, and it appeared by January 1979 that he would be a candidate for president. Early in January, Bush filed with the election panel before he started to collect any money for his campaign. At this point, Bush had some support from the moderate wing of the Republican party. Adam Clymer of the *New York Times* discussed Bush's support in an article on January 6, 1979. "Much of the early support for Mr. Bush has come from the ranks of former Ford partisans," he wrote, "and Mr. Baker discussed his role in the Bush campaign with the former President in November and got his approval."[52] The Mr. Baker discussed was James Baker. He operated Gerald Ford's campaign in 1976, and he would head George Bush's efforts in 1980. Baker and Bush grew closer and would work together in the Reagan administration.

Many viewed Bush as a candidate lacking political skill or as perhaps a stalking horse for Gerald Ford's eventual entry into the race. (Bush took early attacks and then dropped out and threw support to Ford.) Reporters labeled Bush as a moderate and the *Washington Post* felt he was tied to Gerald Ford: "It has been speculated that Ford would back Bush for the nomination if he decided not to run for himself."[53] Bush did not fare well in early Gallup polls, finishing far behind the other contenders. Only a third of the respondents had heard of Bush and a lesser percentage wanted him as the next president. The candidate in front of the pack was Ronald Reagan, followed by several who, like Bush, wanted to be seen as an alternative to Reagan. According to David Broder of the *Washington Post*, many insiders questioned Bush's ability to win an election: "Bush has not won an election since 1968, and faces some skepticism as a vote getter."[54] Bush continued his efforts to raise money and meet the people.

His efforts in raising money earned Bush considerable press coverage. Late in January 1979, he became the first candidate to qualify for federal matching funds. Bush had received at least $5,000 in twenty states through individual contributions not exceeding $250. Bush took pride in this accomplishment, and he believed that "it shows a significant development—that I can draw support from across the country."[55] In January and February, Bush also attempted to expand his supporters by eliminating the moderate label. "Bush told reporters he was very uncomfortable being described as a moderate Republican and preferred to be called a conservative

if he was given any label."[56] Bush was able to get David Keene, an advisor
to Reagan, to join his campaign. Keene was a staunch conservative, and
he told Martin Schram of the *Washington Post* the opinion of many conservatives. Schram wrote "that although Reagan is their first choice there
was some feeling that Reagan may not make it—and that Bush is considered by them as a good second choice."[57] Bush's campaign staff became
even more diverse with the addition of former staffers for George Wallace,
including his campaign manager Charles Snyder. These additions helped
Bush in the South against Reagan and Connally.

In Washington, Bush formally announced his candidacy on May 1, 1979.
The announcement received front page coverage in the national papers.
Adam Clymer of the *New York Times* analyzed Bush's campaign at the
time. "His support has come mainly from the party's moderates, although
few of his stands dismay Republican conservatives."[58] Clymer continued
to look at Bush and the problems he faced in early caucus and primary
states such as Iowa and New Hampshire: "Many of his Iowa backers indicated that their first choice would be to have Gov. Robert D. Ray run as
a favorite son. In New Hampshire, some of his prominent supporters would
really prefer Elliot Richardson, and in many parts of the country, he is the
second choice of adherents of former President Ford."[59]

Nick Thimmesch of the *Washington Post* picked up the theme of Bush
as everyone's second choice for president two days later. "So while Reagan
dominates and Connally climbs, Bush is satisfied to work the country,
county by county, and become everybody's second choice. Being the un-
disputed second man and having fair numbers liking him first, is real
strength, he argues, because it shows my ability to unify."[60] Bush continued
to campaign hard in Iowa and New Hampshire with mixed results.

Polls in the early summer still had Reagan far ahead, with Bush third
trailing John Connally. Prospects might not have appeared good, but Bush
supporters continued to point out that Jimmy Carter had worse numbers
in 1975. Joseph Kraft of the *Washington Post* compared all the candidates
in a column from July 1979. He concluded with a discussion about George
Bush:

Finally, there is George Bush, the former everything. He is working harder than
anybody else. He was the first big name Republican to enter the field. He counts
on a good showing in the Iowa caucuses and the New Hampshire primary to carry
him the rest of the way. The theme of his campaign is the "New Candor." He is,
in other words, a copy of Jimmy Carter in 1976.[61]

Bush continued to be compared to Jimmy Carter, but their campaign
styles were drastically different. While Carter was shaking hands with
everyone possible in Iowa for over a year, Bush met with county officials
to elicit their support. Rowland Evans and Robert Novak compared this

style to Ronald Reagan's approach in Iowa. "Contrasted with Reagan's wholesale politics of monster rallies and massive television, it is a deliberate one at a time courtship requiring immense patience and time."[62] Bush's political future depended on how well his style worked in Iowa.

Most of the candidates for president had announced their intentions by September 1979. Bush was part of a crowded field that included Ronald Reagan, John Connally, Bob Dole, Phil Crane, Howard Baker, and John Anderson. The fact that both Bush and Connally called Texas home could be very important in the race for nomination or in the general election. Columnist Jack Anderson compared both Texans and believed they were long shots for the nomination. "But it's a good bet that one or the other will wind up on the ticket, as the running mate if not the presidential candidate," he wrote.[63] Bush would have to break out of the pack of candidates in Iowa for his candidacy to stand a chance. He hoped to begin this process with a successful speech before the National Press Club.

In his speech, covered by David Broder, "Bush predicted he would do well enough in Iowa and New Hampshire next winter that he would be viewed as a serious challenger to Reagan."[64] Broder continued to discuss Bush in his column several days later. Broder argued that, at the National Press Club, Bush showed that he had done his homework on the issues, but he came to town trailing the question of how a man with such impressive experience and leadership can be as much an unknown to the voters as Bush apparently is."[65] Broder continued saying that Bush's best chance for a Carter-like victory would be in Iowa. A victory or a very good showing by Bush would eliminate other candidates. "His initial struggle for survival is with other 'centrists' in the race, particularly Sens. Howard Baker Jr. of Tennessee and Bob Dole of Kansas. At this point, he is miles ahead of both of them in money and organization, but way behind in public recognition and support."[66]

Bush's popularity did not grow. A *Detroit News* poll in October placed him fifth for the nomination. Although his popularity lagged nationally, his organization won for him two straw votes in Iowa in the fall. Bush received another boost at the end of October, when former President Ford decided that he would not run for president in 1980. Bush believed that Ford's announcement would help his campaign. "There was confusion and the longer Ford's considered candidacy clouded things, that was helpful to Reagan," he said.[67]

Bush's efforts to reduce the field of candidates was assisted by Howard Baker in November. Baker had just formally announced his candidacy, and he expected to win a straw vote in Maine the following week. Baker was so confident that he took a plane load of reporters with him to bask in his victory. Unfortunately for Baker, Bush was better organized and defeated Baker and was given a lot of free media coverage, thanks to his rival. Bush also finished a close third in a straw vote in Florida behind Reagan and

Connally. The fellow Texan spent considerable money in Florida and barely gained his second place showing. After these successes, Broder claimed in his column: "As almost every strategist for the 10 Republican candidates would affirm, George Bush has made better use of 1979 than any of his rivals."[68] Columnist George Will also concluded in November that the race for the nomination was just between two men. "My hunch is that the race may be, indeed closer than most people think to becoming a two-man race, but that the two men are Reagan and Bush."[69]

Events seemed to be moving Bush's way as 1979 turned to 1980. In a book by reporter Aram Bakshian titled *The Candidates* published in early 1980, Bakshian compared all the candidates from both parties in seven areas: leadership, communication, organization, war chest, age/health, marriage/family, and wild card. Bush finished second in his ratings to Ronald Reagan. Bakshian praised Bush for his style of campaigning and his ability to unify: "The old school tie is still good for something after all: it gives George Bush the positive aura of a moderate among moderates without undercutting his standing of a conservative among conservatives."[70] "I also believe he is better qualified than most of his rivals to actually be president."[71]

Bush also benefited early in 1980 from a two-page article in the *Washington Post* by Paul Hendrickson. "Scratch George Bush and you may find an orthodox conservative. Though he despises labels, Bush thinks he is closer to a moderate conservative."[72] Hendrickson wrote this article following one of the final debates in Iowa prior to the caucuses. Ronald Reagan was not present, but Hendrickson got to view the other contenders:

That night in the debate in the Des Moines Civic Center, Robert Dole and John Connally are cards. Phil Crane quotes Brandeis. John Anderson quotes C. Vann Woodward. Howard Baker is full aphorism. And George Bush, sitting on the extreme right, seems what he ever may have been—good old dependable George, not so charismatic maybe, but sure, steady, reliable, experienced, like the boat of State herself, a creation somewhere between Booth Tarkington and Grant Wood, your genuine Beefeater, two dollar Nassau, mahogany Republican. Who wants very badly to be President.[73]

The whole race for Bush focused on his performance in Iowa. Bush and his advisors hoped to finish a strong second. They were stunned with their upset victory over Ronald Reagan. Bush carried Iowa with 33 percent of the vote as compared to Reagan's 27 percent. Howard Baker finished a distant third. The Reagan organization was simply not prepared in Iowa. The turnout in 1980 was five times greater than it was in 1976, and Bush's campaign managers got their supporters out. Bush emerged from Iowa as the media darling with magazine covers and a flood of stories. Reagan had not debated in Iowa and critics viewed this as a terrible mistake. He would, however, debate Bush in New Hampshire. The New Hampshire primary would be the determining factor in Bush's race to the presidency. A Bush victory in New Hampshire could have propelled him to the nomination.

Bush's new celebrity also brought increased scrutiny of his positions. Mark Shields in the *Washington Post* on February 15, 1980, stated, "Even a conservative theologian would have difficulty explaining any profound ideological rift between Reagan and Bush in 1980. There are very few substantive differences, but their stylistic differences are significant."[74] Respected journalists Jack Germond and Jules Witcover shared Shield's opinion on Bush's style. "Bush's reputation as a moderate," they wrote, "was founded largely on stylistic criteria rather than on any close analysis of his positions on economics or national security issues."[75] Bush did spend a critical week after Iowa at home talking to the media and not campaigning in New Hampshire. When Bush returned to New Hampshire with his momentum, he did poorly in a debate with Reagan and the other Republican candidates. Bush was able to schedule a debate alone with Reagan for February 23, 1980. Observers viewed this debate as crucial for both Reagan and Bush.

Just prior to their debate in New Hampshire, Ronald Reagan arrived with four other Republican candidates. The Bush people were against their inclusion. At one point, Reagan grabbed the microphone and claimed that he was paying for this microphone. The crowd rallied behind Reagan, making Bush look bad for refusing the other candidates a chance to debate. Bush never recovered his momentum after this debate fiasco. Reagan defeated Bush in the New Hampshire primary by twenty-seven points, 50 percent–23 percent. Reagan followed up his win with victories in five of the next six primaries. Bush also faced the problem of another candidate stealing some of the spotlight. John Anderson, the little-known congressman from Illinois, began to make noise.

Part of Bush's strategy was to eliminate as much of his competition as quickly as possible. Following Iowa, Bush's strategy appeared to be working. Bush's defeat in New Hampshire and his drop in the polls gave Anderson a chance. He finished second in the Massachusetts and Vermont primaries, and he expected to do well in his own primary in Illinois. Bush found himself again as the underdog and many offered solutions. Evans and Novak believed that a tougher Bush might emerge. They wrote: "Now I know who Bush reminds me of," one Republican told us after their debate. "He acts like Adlai Stevenson." A softer verdict, but in the same vein, came from a member of Bush's own campaign staff. "Too subdued," he said of Bush's performance, referring particularly to his failure to exploit Reagan's lack of experience in foreign and national security issues.[76] Evans and Novak concluded by suggesting that Bush should attack Reagan on the age issue and save his sinking ship.

Bush began to attack Reagan more with limited success. Bush was able to continue his campaign with a victory in Connecticut, but the future appeared dim. Ronald Reagan was closing in on the necessary delegates to ensure his nomination on the first ballot, and Bush did not have the necessary funds to campaign in California and New Jersey. David Keene, political director of the Bush campaign, said his candidate's nomination was "improbable but not impossible."[77] Bush vowed to continue in the hope of defeating Reagan in Pennsylvania and Michigan, raising enough money to continue to the end of the primary season and then persuading delegates not bound to Reagan to switch to him. Broder looked at Bush's campaign in April as it grew closer to the finish line. He praised Bush for his ability in Iowa to project himself as an alternative to Reagan but criticized him for his actions after his victory in Iowa. "The result was that, in the weeks after Iowa, when he had the attention of the public, Bush said nothing to differentiate himself from Reagan," Broder wrote. "And, far from faltering, Reagan delivered his well-memorized lines so perfectly in New Hampshire that he shattered Bush's prized momentum and left him mute and motionless, without theme or direction."[78]

Bush, however, won in Pennsylvania by discussing the economy and then continued on to the Michigan primary. In Michigan on May 20, 1980, Bush won a landslide victory over Reagan by 57–32 percent. Bush's decisive victory was overshadowed by projections from the networks that Reagan had gone over the top with the number of delegates needed to nominate him in Detroit. Bush spent the following day considering whether he would continue to campaign in California, Ohio, and New Jersey. Broder pointed out that many argued that Bush had remained in the race long enough to build up a claim to the vice presidential nomination. He also noted that this "surmise was denied by both Bush and Baker, and those familiar with the candidates thinking said he considers the chances of being tapped by Reagan minimal."[79]

Bush's advisers convinced him that he could not raise the necessary funds to continue. Bush withdrew from the race on May 24, 1980. Bill Peterson covered his press conference for the *Washington Post*. "Bush steadfastly denied interest in the vice presidency and repeated it yesterday in his press conference. But his name can be expected to be more frequently mentioned as a possible Reagan running mate."[80] Bush's two-year struggle for the White House was over. He had the opportunity in Detroit at the Republican National Convention to speak to his supporters, but Bush still found himself the second choice. This did not mean that he should be the Republican party's vice presidential nominee, but it made him a serious contender for Ronald Reagan to consider.

Ronald Reagan had two months to select his running mate. In 1976, Reagan selected moderate Senator Richard Schweiker of Pennsylvania prior to the convention in the hope of drawing delegates away from President

Ford. This time around Reagan had the nomination safely in hand, and he needed someone who would help in the general election. Lou Cannon looked at the Reagan camp's efforts to find a running mate in May for the *Washington Post*. Cannon described how Richard Wirthlin, a Reagan strategist, was conducting a poll to see which candidate helped Reagan the most.

The list of candidates resembled the original list of candidates for the nomination with a few additions. The list included Howard Baker of Tennessee, Jack Kemp of New York, Richard Lugar from Indiana, Paul Laxalt of Neveda, Governor James Thompson of Illinois, John Connally from Texas, and George Bush. Cannon offered his opinion: "No one in the Reagan camp can be found who expects Bush to be Reagan's running mate. Reagan and his aides are concerned about how a running mate would fare in debates with Vice President Mondale, a respected adversary. Baker and Kemp are considered good debaters, while Bush has proven ineffective in a series of debates with Reagan."[81]

Several days before the Republican convention, David Broder, for the *Washington Post*, reported that President Ford was making it clear that he wanted Bush on the ticket with Reagan. This opinion was shared by the level of support Bush had with the delegates.

The chief assets, as they are viewed by Bush supporters in Detroit, are that he showed he could win against the formidable opposition of Reagan, the key states of Michigan, Pennsylvania and Connecticut, that he brings organizational support and that his nomination will be perceived as a reaching out by Reagan to unify the party with a candidate whose views on women's rights differ from his own. Bush also is seen as a hard campaigner.[82]

Broder also reported that Ford would confer with Reagan at the convention about selecting his running mate.

The support of the former president and the delegates seemed to be moving Bush's way, but Reagan had not committed himself to Bush. Evans and Novak attempted to answer this question in their column, "The Trouble with Bush." "The immediate cause for Reagan's stated opposition is one that seldom gets into public debate. He feels that Bush's opposition to an anti-abortion constitutional amendment may well violate Reagan's pledge to the pro life movement to select an anti-abortion running mate."[83] Evans and Novak then added a more personal reason for Reagan's reluctance to select Bush. "But Reagan continues to resist the irresistible for another and more basic reason than the abortion issue. He and Nancy Reagan have made clear to their aides that they simply do not think Bush is up to the presidency, that judgment, highly colored by Bush's performance in New Hampshire, seems an ineradicable mind set."[84]

On Wednesday night, July 16, 1980, George Bush was to speak before

the Republican National Convention. He heard prior to the convention that
the Reagan camp would view the speeches of vice presidential contenders
with great interest. Rumors were flying around Joe Louis Arena in Detroit
and on television throughout the evening that Gerald Ford would be Reagan's running mate. Victor Gold, Bush's speechwriter and adviser discussed
that night on a C-Span retrospective. He said that just before Bush went
to the podium they heard that the Ford deal was completed. Bush's antic-
ipation and excitement dropped, but he was able to give a wonderful speech
attacking Jimmy Carter and praising Ronald Reagan. Bush returned to his
hotel believing that the campaign was over for him.

Following Reagan's nomination, Bush went to bed. Suddenly the phone
rang after 11:30; it was Ronald Reagan asking him to be his running mate.
The deal with Gerald Ford had fallen through. Bush was once again second
choice, but he accepted the offer. Reagan then arrived at the Joe Louis
Arena and announced to the country that George Bush was his choice for
vice president. The following morning Bush and Reagan met with reporters.
The press asked Bush about their differences. Warren Weaver reported
Bush's response for the *New York Times*. "I'm not going to get nickeled
and dimed to death on little details," he said. "What about being Reagan's
second choice?" "What difference does it make?" Bush asked reporters.
"It's irrelevent. I'm here. I believe Gov. Reagan wants me on his ticket."[85]

Bush was nominated the following night, and he and Reagan began their
campaign together. Bush helped Reagan in industrial states such as Michigan and Pennsylvania and also in the suburbs. In the fall, Reagan and
Bush prepared to battle President Carter and John Anderson who decided
to run as an independent. Bush could help Reagan against Anderson by
gaining the support of upperclass Republicans. Many in the media viewed
the political marriage of Reagan and Bush as one of convenience, for they
could not fathom Bush's usefulness.

Reagan sent Bush to China following the convention to help his image
on foreign affairs and his past position against China. Reagan had strongly
condemned China in the past and opposed its gaining a seat in the United
Nations. Bush was well received by his old friends in China and the trip
was a success. On the issue of debates, Carter, Reagan, and Anderson met
in various forums. Often they were controversial because of the candidacy
of Anderson. A debate between George Bush and Walter Mondale was
vetoed by the Reagan camp because they still did not trust Bush's debating
skill after the New Hampshire debate. Bush was to campaign in safe Republican territory and remain noncontroversial. Reagan had substantial
support from conservative Democrats, so it was Bush's responsibility to
keep traditional Republicans in the fold.

Reporters wanted to find out what Bush's role as vice president would
be. Unfortunately, Bush was not sure of his role himself. Bill Peterson of
the *Washington Post* posed this question to Bush. Peterson noted, "He

hasn't bothered to ask Reagan what he would do as vice president." He went on to quote Bush's response. "If I earn the full confidence of Gov. Reagan, I'll have plenty to do. I am what I am. I'm on the ticket because he thought and the convention thought, I could help in some areas."[86] Bush's role was to remain out of trouble. He was questioned about his "voodoo economics" statement he made against Reagan's fiscal policies during the primary season. Bush replied: "God, I wish I hadn't said that."[87]

Bush's role was simply to avoid saying anything to hurt Reagan's chances in November. Reporter Felicity Barringer looked at this role for the *Washington Post* in September. "Let's face it," said press secretary Peter Teeley, "the only way we're going to make national headlines is if we screw up. And we don't want to do that."[88] Bush spent most of his time helping to raise money for state and local campaigns. "This new role doesn't mean that I can't express myself," the candidate said. "But why make the needless mistake anyway."[89]

George Bush and Walter Mondale did not receive much media coverage during the campaign. Reporters and authors who wrote about the contest credit this lack of attention to the campaign of John Anderson. His effort took reporters away from the running mates. Broder did write about another role that Bush gained during the campaign. He quoted a key Pennsylvania suburban county Republican chairman as saying, "The only reason most of our ticket splitters are breaking to Reagan is Bush, they figure that voting for Reagan, they'll eventually get Bush as president, too."[90] In all the literature about this campaign, this was the only instance in which someone mentioned voting for Reagan because George Bush was his running mate.

Just before the election, the *Washington Post* reported that Reagan and Bush had grown closer during the campaign. "If he thinks I fit the description of a person who is supportive and on the team and willing to speak up when I differ with him, he'll listen," said Bush. "And I think he does think that."[91] Karlyn Barker concluded that "Bush is banking on his campaign performance and on Reagan's reputation for delegating authority to ensure that he get some influential duties as vice president."[92] The campaign finally came to an end; it was now up to the voters to decide the fate of George Bush.

Ronald Reagan defeated Jimmy Carter handily at the polls. Bush responded to Reagan's victory with the following statement: "America, in the words of the song, is on the road again—and with the leadership of Ronald Reagan that road is going to lead our country back to greatness."[93] At a joint press conference the day after the election, Reagan was asked what Bush's role would be. Reagan did not give a precise answer, for he was still uncertain about Bush's duties. Bush's role as vice president would evolve after he took the oath of office.

During the interim, from November 1980 to January 1981, the *Wash-*

*ington Post* discussed George Bush's future. Bill Peterson focused on the age issue of Ronald Reagan and how this would effect Bush's vice presidency. "Quite simply, Reagan's age will make Bush's vice presidency different. It will shape the way the new vice president acts and what he does."[94] Ronald Reagan would turn seventy before his inauguration. "No matter how much he protests to the contrary, Bush will find it hard to ignore the prospect that he could rise to the top job in the White House in a few years—or blow it all."[95] Bush had been everyone's second choice for years. He now found himself on January 20, 1981, taking the oath of office for the second highest office in the land. Being the second choice had got him in position to become president. He would have to use the vice presidency carefully and not let himself be destroyed by it to become everyone's first choice for president.

Van Buren and Bush had taken advantage of past experience to reach the vice presidency. Van Buren's use of patrons has been well documented. Bush had used family connections and caught the attention of Richard Nixon and Gerald Ford to rise in politics. Both men now prepared to serve the oldest individuals to hold the presidency up to that time. The health of both chief executives would come into question rather quickly during Van Buren's and Bush's first year in office. Were they prepared to take over?

Bush and Van Buren had spent years in various offices until they became vice president. What had they learned in their pursuit of the vice presidency that would help in their future political endeavors? Both knew the fundamentals of politics from the ground up, even better than the men they prepared to serve as vice president. Bush learned his lessons as the chairman of the Republican National Committee and on the campaign trail for the presidency and vice presidency. Van Buren was regarded at the time, and by historians today, as one of the founders of the Democratic party and instrumental in getting Andrew Jackson elected president in the first place. The experience that both gained along the path to the vice presidency would be helpful when they finally took their careful steps toward the presidency.

# 2

# Avoiding the Dilemma

Through hard work and by being in the right place at the right time, Martin Van Buren and George Bush became vice president and were just one step away from the presidency. Yet, the office of the vice president had lost its importance since the ratification of the Twelfth Amendment in 1804. Van Buren and Bush had to use this office wisely if they planned to follow in the footsteps of Andrew Jackson and Ronald Reagan. This section traces the actions of Van Buren and Bush while they were vice president, in Van Buren's case from inauguration day 1833 until his nomination for president in May 1835, in Bush's case from January 1981 until the autumn of 1987 when he announced his candidacy for the Republican nomination for president.

For Van Buren, this period was far shorter than for George Bush. Van Buren was nominated in May 1835 to prevent any opposition within the Democratic party from forming and because of President Jackson's precarious health. Jackson did not want anyone to argue that Van Buren was not his heir apparent. During his twenty-six months as vice president, Van Buren presided over the Senate while important debates over nullification, the Second Bank of the United States, and Indian removal were taking place. A wrong step could have ruined Van Buren's presidential aspirations. Van Buren also had to contend with being labeled as Jackson's heir apparent. This label not only angered enemies of Van Buren, such as Webster, Clay and Calhoun, but also Jackson supporters such as Senator Hugh White of Tennessee and Davy Crockett. Van Buren's probable candidacy was acceptable in the North, but the South was uncertain about the man forced upon the region by Old Hickory. Van Buren's two years as vice president was a careful balancing act with his every move carefully scrutinized.

George Bush's period as vice president was far longer than Van Buren's. Bush served over six years at the side of Ronald Reagan prior to announcing his candidacy for president. His task was far more complicated than Van Buren's. Bush was not viewed as Reagan's heir apparent. His description of Reagan's fiscal policies as "voodoo economics" continued to haunt the vice president throughout Reagan's two terms. Bush also did not preside over a Senate debating issues of any importance in comparison to those of Van Buren's time. Bush gained visibility by attending ceremonial functions around the world. The decisions of the Reagan administration were not made in close collaboration with the vice president.

Bush's importance rose dramatically during Reagan's reelection bid in 1984. Bush faced no opposition for his renomination, and he was a great help to Reagan during the general election campaign. Reagan appeared old and confused in his first debate with Walter Mondale, which caused a general uneasiness among many Republicans. A poor performance by George Bush might have resulted in panic for the Republican party. Bush's successful debate with Geraldine Ferraro restored confidence, and Reagan's second performance steadied the Republican ship as it cruised to another landslide victory.

Bush spent his second term preparing his path for the 1988 nomination. Bush had to gain the support of Ronald Reagan and keep him neutral during the primary season. Reagan could easily come out and endorse another candidate and steal the nomination from him. Van Buren had the Democratic nomination virtually handed to him; Bush had to fight hard for his. Bush also faced scandal in the Reagan administration. The Iran/Contra affair dominated the last two years of Reagan's presidency. Bush was on a tightrope. Bush denied any knowledge of the scandal, but his denial raised questions about what he had been doing for the past seven years. Bush continued to be haunted by the Iran/Contra affair throughout his campaign for president.

In the end, Van Buren and Bush successfully used the vice presidency to gain their respective party's presidential nominations. The specter of death and assassination hung over the men that Van Buren and Bush hoped to succeed. The nation needed confidence in the man who might step in at any moment. The next section shows how Van Buren and Bush used the vice presidency to advance their political aspirations and how they avoided falling into the dilemma that had ruined other vice presidents. Their paths were not identical, but they were both filled with comparable obstacles and dangers that shaped their runs for the White House.

## REMAINING THE HEIR APPARENT

There was a great deal of celebration in New York after Van Buren's inauguration as Jackson's vice president in March 1833. The *Albany Argus* was pleased with its favorite son, and it predicted the best for Van Buren's future: "His native state appreciates his distinguished merits; the Union will ere long honor him with the first place in the gift of a free and discriminating government."[1] The *Argus* also took the opportunity in the days following the inaugural to discuss how the plans of Webster, Clay, and Calhoun had failed the previous year: "The reelection of general Jackson they could have endured; but to see Mr. Van Buren, whom they had stigmatized and persecuted, so completely vindicated by the triumphant vote of the people, was more than they could bear."[2] The *Argus* reported as well that Webster and Clay did not attend the inaugural celebrations.

With Van Buren now presiding over the Senate, the nation focused on the end of the nullification crisis in South Carolina and on Jackson's continuing battle with the Second Bank of the United States. Van Buren urged caution in dealing with South Carolina and nullification. The issue was the tariff in South Carolina. The state's legislature passed resolutions nullifying the tariff in the state. President Jackson threatened the use of troops to enforce the law. The Jackson administration ultimately allowed Henry Clay to find a compromise solution that allowed both South Carolina and the president to save face.

The Bank of the United States was the major issue of the 1832 presidential campaign. Henry Clay had been a great supporter of the bank and had sponsored its rechartering. Jackson had opposed the bank and vetoed its rechartering in 1832. Jackson's victory over Clay convinced the president that the nation supported his veto and encouraged him to kill what he believed the Second Bank of the United States was, a monster. In his mind, the Second Bank of the United States had tentacles that controlled the economy throughout the country to the detriment of common folk. Jackson attempted to slay the monster during the summer of 1833.

Opposition to Jackson's choice of Van Buren as his successor spread rumors that Van Buren had changed his mind regarding the rechartering. This rumor, however, had no basis of truth. As mentioned earlier, Van Buren began his political career against the rechartering of the First Bank of the United States in 1812. In April 1833, the *Argus* quickly reprinted Van Buren's opinion about the bank from October 1832: "I am unreservedly opposed to a renewal of the United States' bank, and approve of the refusal of the President to sign the bill passed for that purpose at the last session of Congress, as well on account of the unconstitutionality, as the impolicy of its provisions."[3] During the critical summer months when Jackson decided to remove all the federal deposits from the bank, Van Buren and Congress were out of Washington.

Van Buren was home in New York and joined Jackson in a goodwill tour of the Northeast later in the year. Meanwhile, Jackson wrote to Van Buren twice on the bank and his measures against it:

I want your ideas fully on this point, as I am aware that there will be a diversity of opinion in the cabinet, and perhaps a majority against removing the deposits before the meeting of Congress. That they ought to have been removed the moment the Bank postponed the payment of the 3 pr cts. I had no doubt, still as my health is feeble, and life uncertain, and the administration of the Government on my death must devolve on you, I would not wish to do an act of such importance, without your full views upon this important subject.[4]

Jackson was correct in his belief that his cabinet did not unanimously back his policy toward the bank. Jackson had to replace one secretary of the treasury and had to fire another before he had a secretary who would remove the federal deposits. Van Buren supported the president's actions, including the firing of Secretary of the Treasury William Duane. Jackson's firing of Duane set a presidential precedent. Prior to 1833, no cabinet official had ever been fired, and there was much debate over whether the president had the power to remove a cabinet officer without the approval of the Senate. Jackson wrote to Van Buren following the removal of the deposits and Duane's firing on September 29, 1833:

I would be happy to have you here as soon as it will compart with your convenience. Your views are always grateful to me—they are like my own, always based upon the just grounds of the prosperity for our country and the general good. I have therefore a desire that you should be here to aid me in carrying into effect the great work now in execution.[5]

Van Buren returned and had to tolerate brutal attacks made against Jackson in the Senate for his use of executive power. Van Buren remained out of the capital during the high point of the bank war, where a wrong word could have caused him to hurt his position as Jackson's heir apparent. Marquis James, in his biography of Jackson, has dealt directly with this issue: "Having laboriously ascended to the rank of heir apparent, all he need do was hold what was already gained until 1836, granting that General Jackson should retire no sooner."[6] Some observers argue that the Jackson administration had difficulties because Jackson wanted to make sure that Van Buren succeeded him in 1837 or sooner. Jackson would be accused of corrupting the electoral process in his efforts on behalf of Van Buren. Jackson's fight against the Bank of the United States did not harm Van Buren politically for 1836, but the effects of the bank war caused economic problems for America after Van Buren became president.

Jackson planned a goodwill tour of the Northeast for the summer of 1833. Van Buren was in New York and intended to join the president along the route. The vice president was criticized by some in the press for being out of Washington and for his plans to join the president on his tour. When the tour began in late May, reports of Jackson's poor health were prevalent. By the end of June, Van Buren finally joined the president in New York City. They were met with great applause and enthusiasm, but Jackson's physical condition did not improve.

Finally, in early July, Jackson was forced to bed, and many feared his imminent demise. Reports from the South, printed in the *Argus*, indicated that some were not happy with Jackson's selection of Van Buren as his heir: "After the reins of power have passed the hands of general Jackson, we do not believe that his wishes as to the successor will be more regarded than if he was a beggar expiring on a dung-hill."[7] Jackson's health improved, but reports surfaced from New York City that during Jackson's tour he had narrowly escaped serious injury on several occasions. In one incident, a bridge collapsed just after Jackson and his procession passed over it. Van Buren's elevation to the presidency could be imminent and the criticism of him continued. The *Argus* reprinted from the *Winchester Virginian* the opinion of how harsh this treatment of Van Buren was. "No man has been more persecuted and abused, except the Apostle of Republicanism, Thomas Jefferson."[8]

For most Americans, Martin Van Buren was not as well known as the war hero Andrew Jackson. Most did not personally object to Van Buren, but they did object to President Jackson becoming personally involved in the selection of his successor. Accompanying Jackson on his tour was a great opportunity for Van Buren, and the *Argus* explained why the opposition was so opposed to Van Buren's involvement:

They are well aware that whenever the people shall become acquainted with this distinguished son of New York, the prejudices which it has along been their object to create against him will be dissipated, that when the people of the Union generally shall have an opportunity for judging for themselves of his character by personal observation, they will esteem his private worth and virtues, as much as they have heretofore admired his talents.[9]

The next year was a relatively quiet one for Van Buren. The opposition tried its best to print articles discussing Van Buren's supposed opposition within the Jackson administration. Having failed to stir up trouble in this effort, critics returned to personal attacks against him. They charged him with telling Jackson to remove the bank's deposits by using his magical powers on the old General. As usual the *Albany Argus* came to Van Buren's defense. "His unprecedented success as Secretary of State, in our foreign negotiations, has gained for him the reputation of a statesman that is truly enviable," the paper wrote.[10] The *Argus* then dispelled Van Buren's use of magical powers: "He has the foresight to see what would best promote the interests of the country, and he has the talent and abilities to cope successfully with foreign powers—this is all the magic he has used."[11]

Finally toward the end of 1833, the opposition to Jackson and Van Buren began to discuss possible presidential candidates for 1836. Names such as Senator Daniel Webster of Massachusetts and Judge John McLean of Ohio emerged. Every person mentioned took a secondary place to the man from Kentucky, Henry Clay. In the end, Clay chose not to run for president in 1836, but for the next year and a half, the potential candidacy of Clay was always in the background.

For Van Buren, 1834 was the year that his candidacy for president was accepted by most supporters of President Jackson. Attacks continued, but now they focused on his run for president in 1836. Reports surfaced that Van Buren was courting the Catholic vote for 1836. In actuality, this report stemmed from a courteous letter Van Buren had properly written to the future Pope while he was secretary of state. Attacks were leveled against Van Buren for his flip-flopping and noncommittal stance on the issues. One harsh critic was Davy Crockett. He told one story of two men listening to Van Buren speaking about the tariff. After Van Buren completed his speech, the story went, the two men complimented the speech, but they disagreed about which side of the tariff issue Van Buren was supporting. Crockett's attacks evolved into a biography of Van Buren that was used during the 1836 campaign.

From supporters of Van Buren came articles that could have damaged his campaign. The articles supported Van Buren, but they made suggestions regarding his running mate, which could cause hostility prior to the convention. Democratic party leaders in many states accepted Van Buren's nomination but wanted to have a say in who his running mate would be. Jackson selected Van Buren and the party wanted to select his vice president. Other than this minor concern, Van Buren's future appeared bright. The *Argus* noted why Van Buren would be the best candidate to carry on Jackson's policies in a story in 1834: "The displays of affection and confidence that reach us from every quarter, clearly indicate that the democracy of the Union look to Mr. Van Buren as the next connecting link in that chain of republican statesmen, by whom their principles are to be, it is hoped, eternally sustained."[12]

As the year drew to a close, it became obvious that Van Buren would be a candidate for the presidency in 1836. Questions surrounding his running mate and what the opposition would do in 1836 remained. Thomas Hart Benton, the powerful senator from Missouri, wrote in December 1834 how bitter the attacks against Van Buren had been. "No public man, since the days of Mr. Jefferson has been pursued with more bitterness than Mr. Van Buren," he observed, "none, not excepting to Mr. Jefferson himself, has ever had to withstand the combined assaults of so many, and such formidable powers."[13]

Everything was moving toward the Democratic Convention scheduled to meet in Baltimore in May 1835, when an incident occurred that could have changed everything. On January 30, 1835, President Jackson was attending a funeral of a former general. Upon leaving the memorial service, Jackson was met by a man, Robert Lawrence, who aimed two pistols at the president from only a few feet away. Lawrence attempted to fire both pistols, but the gunpowder failed to ignite. Had the pistols worked, Jackson would have been seriously injured, if not killed. Surprisingly, newspapers mentioned nothing about Van Buren and the possibility of him taking over had Jackson been killed. Perhaps since no president had died in office yet, people were not sure what would happen if tragedy occurred. When William Henry Harrison died in 1841, John Tyler's accession to the presidency did not occur without controversy.

Talk continued regarding the upcoming convention and the election the following year. In March, the presidential candidacy of Judge Hugh Lawson White of Tennessee was announced. White was a supporter of Jackson and had been offered the position of secretary of war on two occasions. White broke with Jackson over his use of executive power. He did not approve of Jackson running for reelection in 1832 after he promised to serve only one term. White likewise did not approve of Jackson selecting his heir. White's candidacy could potentially damage Van Buren in Tennessee and throughout the South. This concern aside, the two months prior to the Democratic convention saw a period of praise for Van Buren. The *Argus* denied any wrongdoing by Van Buren throughout his career. "The object of your vindictive attacks remains unscathed. He stands aloof, and unapproachable to your assaults, he rather gains strength from your hostility, like the pure diamond which shines brighter, the more it is rubbed."[14] Van Buren was ready to be nominated for president by the Democratic party, which he had helped to create eight years earlier to elect Andrew Jackson.

The debate over his running mate, however, continued. President Jackson told the delegates that he wanted Senator Richard M. Johnson of Kentucky to run with Van Buren. Johnson's claim to fame was that he had shot and killed the great Shawnee chief Tecumseh at the Battle of the Thames during the War of 1812. John Carton, the chief justice of Tennessee, questioned Jackson's selection in a letter to the president: "Military success has only been taken as evidence of fitness here and the world over and I pray you to assure our friends that the humblest of us do not believe that a lucky random shot even if it hit Tecumseh, qualifies a man for Vice President."[15]

Van Buren's old ally in Virginia, Thomas Ritchie, editor of the *Richmond Enquirer*, also questioned Johnson's selection. In a letter to Virginia's Senator William Rives, Ritchie explained that he wanted Rives and not Johnson on the ticket with Van Buren. "I have freely told and written my friends that with your name associated on the ticket I think Virginia and the South will be safe, with Col. Johnson less than safe."[16] Johnson had some personal problems that concerned many Southerners, including Ritchie. These problems focused on Johnson's relationship with slave women. The only possible stumbling block as the convention approached was the selection of Richard Johnson as Van Buren's running mate. In April 1835, the *Argus* printed its most favorable statement about Van Buren and his candidacy:

General Jackson is intimately acquainted with the principles and characters of all the Presidential candidates, and he considers Mr. Van Buren the best qualified of them all to take his place, it is the strongest recommendation that a gentleman can have, and one which will not be lost upon the American people. If General Jackson does give his preference to Mr. Van Buren it is for the same reason that a great majority of the country also prefers him—for his stern integrity and his uncompromising democratic principles—and because in his election, the people have the fullest assurance, that the measures and policy of the present administration will be fully carried out.[17]

Martin Van Buren was the unanimous choice of the delegates attending the Democratic convention in Baltimore. However, the nomination of Richard Johnson posed a little more difficulty. Many supported candidates with sectional appeal and perhaps the capability of gaining votes for the ticket in areas where Van Buren was weak. Many delegates from the South supported other candidates for vice president, especially Virginia Senator William Rives. Jackson had enough delegates in the North and the West to get Johnson nominated. When it was announced to the convention that Johnson had received the nomination, the delegation from Virginia hissed and made it clear that Virginia would refuse to support Johnson the following year. But Johnson was popular in the West and more than a year before the general election, the ticket that Andrew Jackson wanted to succeed him was in place.

Van Buren had not failed in his role as heir apparent, as John C. Calhoun had done previously. Van Buren was a quiet vice president, not publicly involved in the major issues of the day. While in the Senate, Van Buren remained calm, even when President Jackson was under attack for his use of executive power. He had worked for a long time to gain the confidence and trust of Jackson, and he did not jeopardize this position in his first two years as vice president.

But he still had the campaign ahead of him. The next sixteen months would decide whether having Jackson's blessing was enough to succeed him. The opposition to Jackson had loosely come together to form the Whig party. It had not nominated a candidate to run in 1836, and Henry Clay was still lurking in the wings. Van Buren's course appeared clear to the presidency, but a problematic running mate and the presidential candidacy of Hugh White could hurt Van Buren particularly in the South.

There was still the possibility that Van Buren might become president before March 1837 because of the death of Jackson. His ill health remained a factor for the year and a half that Van Buren would campaign for president. Would Van Buren's campaign run as smoothly if Andrew Jackson was suddenly out of the picture? He had made Van Buren his heir apparent and selected his running mate. Many Jackson supporters disagreed with the president's actions but remained loyal to his wishes. This loyalty might evaporate if Jackson succumbed prior to the election.

## TRYING TO BECOME HEIR APPARENT

George Bush had similar problems. He became vice president on January 20, 1981. His years of hard work and loyalty had finally paid off. He was now only a step away from the presidency, and there was a good possibility that President Reagan would serve just one term. Bush's biographer Nicholas King pointed out this opportunity prior to the inauguration. "As Vice President, Bush, a politician who demonstrated his vigor with daily jogging, could look forward with a measure of confidence to being President Reagan's heir presumptive, if not heir apparent, during the four years of a Reagan administration."[18] Bush could use his years as vice president to get closer to the man he had known, but not well, for sixteen years. Bush could develop a good relationship with Reagan as Van Buren developed his tie to Andrew Jackson. Bush also had many supporters from his own unsuccessful campaign. Polling suggested that almost 9 percent of those who voted for Reagan did so because George Bush was on the ticket. King offered an explanation for this phenomenon as well. "Bush's name represents an insurance policy. If something were to happen to Reagan, a younger man of trust, experience and known judgment would be standing by."[19] Little did anyone know that this scenario might occur soon.

Bush quickly fell into the quiet role of vice president following the inaugural. His exposure was limited until March, when his role expanded in the Reagan administration. Reporter Martin Schram for the *Washington Post* reported on Bush's appointment to head crisis management in the White House. "This assignment will amount to an unprecedented role for the vice president in modern time."[20] Schram continued to discuss how the appointment of Bush dismayed some in the White House, especially Secretary of State Alexander Haig. Schram discussed how the president came to his decision. "Bush's stature," he wrote, "by virtue of job title and experience, was cited as the reason that he was chosen to chair meetings in the Situation Room in time of crisis."[21]

David Broder discussed Bush's growing role and influence in an extensive article in the *Washington Post* on March 30, 1981. In his two-page article, Broder stated: "The vice president has become an influential insider in Ronald Reagan's administration."[22] Broder discussed how Bush had expanded his role by meeting regularly with members of Congress and the Republican party, as well as being appointed to chair meetings during a crisis. Bush was made aware of every decision, according to Broder, and each week Bush had a private meeting with the president. In cabinet meetings, Bush offered no opposition to Reagan's ideas. "By every account, Bush's role has grown in proportion to Reagan's confidence in his loyalty and ability—and the personal warmth that has melted previous suspicions."[23] Bush was also expected to take on the brunt of campaigning for Republican candidates.

Bush seemed comfortable in his role as loyal follower of Ronald Reagan. Bush said, "I'm convinced that people will write the Whatever Happened to George Bush? story, and then that's good . . . because if I'm out there high profile, trying to grab credit . . . that would quickly undermine whatever utility I have to the president."[24] The day that this article was printed, Americans spent the afternoon and evening in front of their televisions. Ronald Reagan and three others were shot in an assassination attempt. George Bush was closer to the presidency than anyone could have imagined.

On that horrible Monday, Bush was in Texas speaking in support of Reagan's economic policies when he learned of the shooting. After he was informed that the president had been wounded, Bush made his way back to Washington. His quiet return to the White House was far better organized than the chaotic scene in the White House following the attempt on Reagan's life. Alexander Haig's aggressive attitude and his declaration that he was in charge haunted the secretary of state until his resignation. Bush remained calm, and after Reagan made it out of surgery, he talked to the nation. "I can assure the nation and watching world that this government is functioning fully and effectively."[25]

Bush spent the next couple of weeks while Reagan was in the hospital performing the president's ceremonial duties. Reagan's chief of staff James Baker approved of Bush's performance. "Bush is performing extremely well. He's filling in for the president without being brash or overly assertive. I speak for everybody here."[26] Apparently the nation also approved of Bush's actions. In a *Washington Post*/ABC News poll, 68 percent of those polled believed that Bush could handle the job of president as opposed to only 15 percent who believed he could not.[27]

Reagan made a relatively quick recovery, and Bush returned to his background role by attending the Major League All Star game and traveling overseas. In 1981, Bush visited France and Latin America. As the year drew to a close, Broder studied Bush's first year in office for the *Washington Post*.

In his first year on the job, Bush has experienced at least his full quota of the usual vice presidential ups and downs. Shunted into the sideline area of regulatory reform during the rush to launch the administration's tax and budgetary cuts, he was thrust to the forefront by his calm circumspect performance during the anxious hours and days after Reagan was shot.[28]

Broder also focused on Bush's decision not to dissent in cabinet meetings. Bush explained his feelings: "It is an absolute determination not to express myself. Suppose several Cabinet members, or even one Cabinet member, expresses a view, and I express a contrary view. I don't think the president should ever have to choose between me and a Cabinet member. That's not the way to have a relationship of confidence."[29]

Broder argued that Bush had gained some support from conservatives since January, and with Richard Bond's appointment as deputy chairman of the Republican National Committee, the future appeared bright for Bush. Bond had run Bush's successful 1980 campaign in Iowa, and staunch conservatives opposed this appointment. Bush could possibly succeed Reagan in 1985 or 1989, and Bond's appointment was proof that the president was not dissatisfied with his vice president. Bond's position could help Bush considerably in gaining the nomination in 1984 or 1988.

George Bush did an excellent job in his first year as vice president. He was calm during the days following the assassination attempt and he appeared capable of becoming president. He believed that he had gained the trust of the president with his appointment as crisis leader and by getting Bush supporters such as James Baker and Richard Bond in positions of influence. The next several years offered fewer opportunities. There would not be daily horseback rides with Reagan that Van Buren enjoyed with Andrew Jackson, but Bush did use his weekly luncheons with the president to share his opinions with Reagan.

Bush's second year as vice president found him virtually invisible until the fall of the year. Bush traveled to Asia and Africa and to Moscow for Leonid Breznhev's funeral, but he kept a low profile. The only real excitement for Bush came in February 1982, when a brick struck his car on the way to the White House. It was originally reported that this might have been an assassination attempt against Bush. The Secret Service was protective following the attempt on Reagan's life, and it conducted an extensive search of the scene looking for terrorists. However, investigation by the Secret Service and the D.C. police concluded that the brick accidentally fell from a construction site and was not an assassination attempt.

Bush remained out of sight, and a young boy in Maine wanted to know where he was. The *Washington Post* printed the story in February. Eight-year-old Derek Adams wrote to a local newspaper in Maine. "I haven't been hearing about George Bush lately. Did he quit his job, or did he die?

Do you know?"[30] This letter was passed on to the vice president, who wrote back to the young boy that he was alive and explained why he had been unnoticed lately: "It is my belief that I can serve the president best in a quiet way," he wrote. He also noted that vice presidents "usually don't receive a lot of attention in the media."[31]

Another story in the spring gave the credit for Bush's nomination to his campaign manager James Baker. Columnists James Dickerson and David Broder discussed this in a piece for the *Washington Post*. The article makes the case that Bush became vice president thanks to Baker, who was now Reagan's chief of staff. Baker, they said, claimed that it was he who forced Bush to withdraw before the California primary in 1980 against his wishes by announcing that the Bush campaign lacked funds to continue. Bush opposed withdrawing because he did not want to be seen as a quitter. According to Dickerson and Broder, Baker explained: "He was not particularly popular with Gov. Reagan. If George had further alienated him back then by entering a primary in Gov. Reagan's home state as a pure spoiler, there is no way he'd be where he is."[32] This article placed more importance on Baker's contribution in getting Bush nominated than the fact that the convention delegates supported Bush and that Gerald Ford turned down the nomination and continued to support the addition of George Bush to Ronald Reagan's ticket.

Mid-term elections took place in 1982, and Bush did substantial campaigning for Republican candidates. This year was also the beginning of talks about 1984. Ronald Reagan was now well over seventy years of age and had survived an assassination attempt. Many doubted that he would run for reelection; attention, therefore, turned to George Bush. Humorist Art Buchwald looked at Bush in September and described his predicament following a discussion with a mythical Bush supporter. "He has been vice president of the United States for two years, so nobody knows who he is. In fact, people haven't heard from him in so long that many who supported him think he's dropped out of the public life."[33] The Bush supporter agreed with Buchwald: "I'll tell you one thing. Being vice president of the United States doesn't do anything for a person's political image."[34] This supporter also realized the dilemma that would face Bush if he ran for president while remaining vice president. "Every vice president who has run for president has been in trouble because he was too closely associated with his boss. We'd like to avoid that with Bush if we could."[35] But 1982 was not the year for Bush to separate himself from Reagan because he was the principal defender of the administration during the mid-term campaign.

Bush was the principal campaigner for the Reagan administration because, following the attempt on his life, the president continued to take a backseat when it came to campaigning. In addition, other leading Republicans were preparing their paths for 1984 and 1988 and would not spend their time supporting the actions of the Reagan administration. Bush traveled over 70,000 miles in the United States campaigning for Reagan and Republican candidates, but he was viewed as an unexciting campaigner and some suggested that he should become a tougher supporter of the candidates he endorsed.

Republicans feared that they might lose control of the Senate and lose the coalition in the House of Representatives that was able to pass much of Reagan's domestic agenda. Bush feared potential losses as well, but he would not change his style of campaigning. Bush made this statement in October in a column by Broder: "I'm not Spiro Agnew. I'm determined to maintain control of my own campaigning. Sure, you get more attention if you take the colorful hatchman kind of approach, and promise the press some startling prose in every speech. But I'm afraid I'm not that flamboyant."[36] The Republican party maintained control of the Senate, but lost over twenty seats in the House. Bush did an excellent job for candidates running for state offices, which would benefit his efforts in 1988, but that was still a long way off.

On the world stage, 1983 was a big year for Bush. Reports in January said that Bush would be going to Europe to help explain the Reagan administration's nuclear weapons policies to European leaders. In her article on January 11, Mary McGrory of the *Washington Post* wanted to know where Bush had been prior to his departure:

The vice president has, in recent months, all but disappeared from the public view, which of course is what vice presidents are supposed to do. Heirs apparent provide unwelcome reminders of presidential mortality, and Bush, whose record of self-effacement is impeccable, has been made to feel that he must do even more in this regard because of the rage the sight of him stirs in the right wing.[37]

Bush was well received in Europe, although the nuclear policies of Ronald Reagan were not. Reporter Michael Getler covered the vice president in Europe, and he discussed how good Bush was in his meetings with the other leaders debating President Reagan's zero-zero plan regarding placing weapons in Europe: "The vice president, who by choice dwells largely in the shadows of this administration, carried off a tricky appointment for the president at a particularly sensitive time in U.S.-European relations. Such a demonstration of his skills can only help Bush inside the administration, and could conceivably enhance his political future as well."[38] Bush had to dispel the image of Reagan in Europe as a gunslinging cowboy unwilling to reach a compromise. Getler argued that Bush had done just that. He said, "Bush no doubt reassured Europe while enhancing the image of the administration."[39]

Bush returned to Europe in June and was met by protesters in Germany, but for the rest of the year, the vice president's attention focused on national politics. Ronald Reagan did not announce in 1983 that he was running for reelection, so Bush had to keep his own foot in the door for 1984. He hoped to do so by moving closer to the right wing of the Republican party. Juan Williams for the *Washington Post* discussed Bush's endorsement as vice president by the Reverend Jerry Falwell, founder of the Moral Majority, in May. Bush visited Falwell's Liberty Baptist College and tried to downplay his preppy Yale image. Bush put on a Liberty Baptist tie and received a standing ovation from the student audience. "That scene was a high point for Bush in his two and a half years as No. 2 in the government," Williams wrote, "a sign that the staunch right wing opposition that has dogged him so long and clouded his chances to be president may be softening."[40]

Williams also discussed the strong support that President Reagan was showing for his vice president. "Last week, in an unusually strong endorsement with the 1984 nominating convention still more than a year away. Pres. Reagan said that 'when I needed someone of unquestionable leadership, loyalty, and skill there is only one person I could or would choose again, and that's my partner and your vice president.' "[41] Reagan continued his praise of Bush: "I don't think that I can recall many vice presidents who have been involved and much a part of things as he has."[42] Even so, many questions about Bush remained within the Republican party.

Lyn Notzinger, a Republican strategist and a close aide to Reagan in 1980, opposed Bush's selection and did not believe that Bush would gain the party's nomination without a fight in 1984 if Reagan chose not to run. Nofzinger stated, "Bush has been loyal and done a good job as vice president. The question is what does he believe. No one knows what George Bush has been thinking or doing. He's been low profile. You don't know that he's a Reaganite."[43] Bush had been successful in submerging his differences with Reagan before becoming vice president and had gained his trust and loyalty. Staunch Reagan supporters were still suspicious of George Bush, but as George Will stated in October, "He is the most comprehensively experienced person to serve as vice president. This is a political asset because of Reagan's age. That was expected to be an issue in 1980 and was not. It is not expected to be in 1984, but may be. Perhaps it will be less an issue than a vague anxiety. If so, Bush and his many credentials will be important again."[44]

Bush did have another role as vice president that had not received much attention—his position as president of the Senate. Van Buren had earlier presided over a Senate that discussed very important issues with members who had presidential ambitions. Bush rarely presided over such a Senate, but in one instance in 1983, he had to break a tie in order for the United States to continue producing nerve gas. This controversial vote upset many Bush supporters, including his mother. Reagan called her to reassure her that George's vote would not hurt his political future.

Bush faced 1984 in a much stronger position than he had been four years earlier. He was vice president and he already had the endorsement of Ronald Reagan and Jerry Falwell to continue in his office if the president chose to run for reelection. There was no organized effort to replace him like the efforts of 1944 and 1956 to replace Henry Wallace and Richard Nixon. Bush was firmly secured in his number two position. Questions remained concerning Bush's presidential ambitions, but that probably would not come into focus in 1984. Bush had performed well on the world stage and in gaining Reagan's trust, but the right wing would continue to look at him suspiciously. Still, Bush had to wait for Reagan's decision to see where his future lay.

Ronald Reagan finally ended speculation by announcing late in January that he would be a candidate for reelection in 1984. In his brief statement to the nation, Reagan mentioned his vice president. "We have made a new beginning. Vice President Bush and I would like to have your support and cooperation in completing what we began three years ago."[45] The die had finally been cast. George Bush would run again for vice president, and he quickly returned to the campaign trail for Ronald Reagan. Bush was the principal campaigner during the primary season, and he offered this testament to Reagan in New Hampshire in mid-February. "We found a president whose optimism about our country and its fundamental values and its future never wavered—a leader with the courage to make the tough decisions and see them through."[46]

Bush enjoyed a powerful role during the early phase of the campaign. Lou Cannon of the *Washington Post* looked at Bush's actions and what they could mean for his future. "After three years of anonymity, Vice President Bush has emerged as President Reagan's chief surrogate in foreign policy crisis and his political point man in the developing presidential election campaign."[47] Cannon explained that much of Bush's influence was because of Reagan's chief of staff, James Baker. He concluded, "At 59, Bush owes much to Reagan. One thing is Reagan's virtual redefinition of the age issue in national politics. If Bush ran and was elected in 1988, he would be nearly seven years younger than Reagan was when he was inaugurated."[48]

Bush continued his efforts for Reagan but had time to attend Yuri Andropov's funeral in the Soviet Union and to visit Pakistan. The strength of Reagan's presidency was foreign policy, and Bush was able to emphasize his foreign policy experience as well on his trips. Bush returned to the United States and began his preparations for the Republican National Convention. He arrived this time not needing to gain a spot on the ticket, but ready to perform well enough so that next time he could be accepting the party's presidential nomination.

Bush's upcoming performance was discussed by Dale Russakoff for the *Washington Post*. He argued that Bush had come a long way since 1980, "boasting four years of unflagging fealty to a man he once opposed on

basic issues of foreign policy, women's rights and the economy."[49] Reagan
and Bush faced Walter Mondale and his running mate Geraldine Ferraro
in the general election. A debate between the running mates was being
discussed, although many in the Reagan camp had not forgotten Bush's
performance in New Hampshire four years earlier. Russakoff discussed this
possibility a few days later. "If Bush debates his performance in that highly
charged and sensitive contest is not likely to be forgotten by 1988, particularly if he is perceived as losing it."[50] Bush had clearly won Reagan over,
but now he would have to attempt to win the party over.

Mary McGrory covered Bush at the convention and compared the applause received by Bush and Jack Kemp, the former Buffalo Bills Quarter-
back and now the New York congressman. McGrory reported that Kemp's
applause was more enthusiastic. Kemp was the darling of the conservative
wing of the party, and many believed that he was the true ideological heir
to Ronald Reagan. McGrory admitted that Bush had gained some support
from the right since becoming vice president. "Bush has been it is true, an
exemplainary self effacing vice president," she noted. "It is also true that
he redeemed himself somewhat by breaking tie votes in the Senate on chem-
ical warfare and twice on the MX missile system dear to Tory hearts."[51]
McGrory concluded that the election outcome looked good for Reagan and
Bush, but the vice president still had to debate Geraldine Ferraro. "Nobody
here thinks that Ferraro can turn it around for the Democrats. But she had
the power to rock George Bush's dreamboat."[52] Their debate was scheduled to take place in Philadelphia on October 12, 1984, sandwiched between the two Reagan-Mondale debates.

This second vice presidential debate in American history took on greater
importance after Reagan's first debate with Walter Mondale. In the Lou-
isville debate, Reagan appeared old and confused with facts and figures.
Time ran out on Reagan. During his closing remarks, Reagan was in the
middle of a story about driving on the Pacific Coast Highway. He had
performed badly. Pressure shifted to Bush to steady the Republican campaign. A poor performance by Bush could shrink Reagan's lead over Mondale and make the campaign competitive again. The public might give
Mondale and Ferraro a chance.

Bush performed wonderfully that evening in Philadelphia. He displayed
his command of the facts, and he showed that he possessed far more knowledge about foreign policy than Ferraro. In discussing the debate, syndicated
columnist Al Hunt believed that "Bush clearly was in charge of his facts
and his erratic behavior settled down as the debate progressed. Generally
he was neither too passive nor too aggressive."[53] When questioned about
voicing his difference with Reagan, Bush answered carefully. "I couldn't
do that to Ronald Reagan, now, next year or any other time. I have too
much trust in him. And I'd feel very uncomfortable doing that."[54] Bush
concluded his closing statement by defending his role as vice president and

his attitude of not disagreeing with the president. "I owe my president my judgment and then I owe him loyalty. You can't have the president of the United States out there looking over his shoulder wondering whether his vice president is going to be supporting him."[55]

Polls taken following the debate showed that a majority of Americans believed that Bush had won. The following day Bush was overheard by reporters saying that "we tried to kick a little ass last night." Bush apologized for the remark, but some commentators believed that this remark and an earlier statement by Barbara Bush were calculated. Mrs. Bush had said that "Ferraro was a word that rhymed with witch." "These slips may have been intentional efforts to show the patrician second family as down to earth, real people."[56] Republicans praised George Bush, but the press took another view for the remainder of the campaign.

The press became highly critical of Bush following his debate with Ferraro. Joseph Kraft in the *Washington Post* argued that Bush remade himself to appease the right of his party:

The point, plainly, is to show Bush as a tough gut fighter amenable to the Republican right. But the pose won't fool the right wingers. They knew that Bush comes from the wrong schools and practices the wrong brand of religion. But the rest of the country knows what it sees and hears. So unless the real George Bush stands up, the general impression will be a foolish fellow unfit to be president.[57]

Ronald Reagan came to Bush's defense during his successful second debate with Walter Mondale. When asked about Bush, Reagan had these words about his vice president: "George Bush, . . . who I think is one of the finest vice presidents this country has had."[58] Reagan and Bush had steadied their campaign, and it was apparent by late October that only the size of the landslide was in question. Since the Republican convention, Bush did not receive the coverage that his counterpart enjoyed. Ferraro was followed by people and reporters everywhere she campaigned. Bush was forced to run a quiet campaign, and his aides were looking along with him to 1988. Bush would not discuss 1988 until after the election. He would remain the loyal supporter, or lackey, of Ronald Reagan, depending on one's viewpoint.

The expected landslide occurred: Reagan lost only Minnesota and the District of Columbia to Walter Mondale. George Bush prepared to serve another four years at Reagan's side and began facing questions regarding 1988. According to Dale Russakoff of the *Washington Post*, "Throughout the campaign Bush was under scrutiny not only as the understudy to President Reagan, but also as a presidential contender in waiting."[59] Discussions of 1988 were put off, but most of Bush's aides believed that there would be a presidential effort in four years. "They say," Russakoff wrote, "that the frustrations of 1984 will fade by then and that Bush will be remembered mainly as a faithful Reaganite who won a high stakes debate with Ferraro at a time when the president was smarting over his loss of the first debate with Mondale."[60]

What were Bush's frustrations in 1984? According to political scientist Austin Rainey's study of the elections of 1984, Bush's problems focused on the press. "The press corps following Bush became contemptuous of the vice president during the campaign, considering him weak and wimpish."[61] Bush was attacked harshly by the press, and one can understand why Bush avoided questions about 1988. Bush had survived reelection and was in the lead for the 1988 nomination, but his path was not clear. He was not presented as Reagan's heir apparent yet, and much opposition remained on the right. Bush was also vice president and would have to contend with a century and a half of history in order to claim the presidency. Lyn Nofziger discussed Bush and the 1988 campaign following the election: "George Bush is going to have to go out and win the presidency. Being vice president doesn't automatically guarantee you the nomination. There are an awful lot of Republicans who will want to challenge him."[62]

In some ways, Bush found himself in 1985 in the same place as in 1980. He would have to remain close to Reagan and cultivate his relationship with the right. The difference for Bush was that Reagan would not be running for another term in 1988. Bush would have to pick the right moment to begin discussing where he would take the country following Reagan. Bush could go too far away from Reagan and lose his support and potential status as heir apparent or remain too close and lose the respect of party leaders and the public if something went wrong with the Reagan administration. Other Republicans could begin planning for 1988 without having to consider the dilemma facing Bush.

In the beginning of 1985, as in 1981, Bush was the focus of questions concerning the next presidential election. There was a discussion that Bush was beginning the job of organizing for 1988, a job difficult for a vice president according to Dale Russakoff. "If he decides to run he would move to articulate his own vision for the nation's future—a task that former vice president Richard M. Nixon, Hubert M. Humphrey and Walter F. Mondale found daunting."[63] Bush explained what he believed he should do prior to 1988: "I think you have to visibly portray your vision for the future and where you want to see the country go. That's way down the road, but I can see positing positions for the future that give people a sort of insight."[64]

Bush was given a large gala prior to the inauguration and was deemed after the inaugural by Dale Russakoff to be the loyal subordinate. In this article, Bush discussed his feelings toward Reagan. "I feel totally relaxed with the man. I'm going to keep supporting him. It's not going to change in any way. . . . He's very gracious. I don't think there's ever been a vice president in history who's ever been treated with that kind of personal regard from the president."[65] On his future political aspirations, "Bush said that he does not expect Reagan to endorse him in 1988, "and I wouldn't ask."[66] Bush was apparently ready for another term as a loyal vice president.

In late March, Bush went on an extensive ten-day tour, traveling about 29,000 miles. He traveled from Africa with Jerry Falwell and the equally conservative Pat Robertson to Moscow for Soviet leader Konstantine Chernenko's funeral and was the first American to meet Mikhail Gorbachev, the new Soviet leader. Following their meeting in Moscow, Bush flew to Central America. The trip was a success for the vice president. His ability to go on these important foreign journeys without any difficulties helped to solidify his position as Reagan's heir.

Bush returned home and once again the press looked at the vice president with 1988 in mind. In April, Bush organized a political action committee (PAC) to help Republican candidates and eventually himself. Bush seemed to be positioning himself as the logical successor to Reagan. In a column in May, Evans and Novak discussed Bush's actions and 1988. " 'I think the nomination is his to lose,' a Bush aide told us, unconsciously repeating the exact words used endlessly by Mondalites in the years preceding 1984."[67] Evans and Novak cautioned Bush against running too cautious a campaign. "As demonstrated by Richard Nixon and Hubert Humphrey, a sitting vice president has little margin for straying from his president—a partial explanation of why Martin Van Buren was the last incumbent vice president elected."[68] Other candidates had the freedom to operate their campaigns without the shadows of Richard Nixon and Hubert Humphrey cast over them.

One of these candidates was Pierre DuPont of Delaware, who discussed the problems of Bush's campaign in a speech in Michigan, as described by Evans and Novak in June 1985. "He did signal where the vice president's potential troubles would be. He warned that Richard Nixon's call for 'eight more years' in 1960 was a message of the past and not a message of hope. Adding that a similar appeal would not work in 1988."[69]

Bush's quiet work continued until President Reagan had his yearly physical in July. Doctors found polyps in his colon that could be cancerous and had to be removed. Before undergoing surgery, Reagan notified Congress on July 13, 1985, that he would be unable to discharge his duties as president and power was passed to George Bush for eight hours. Bush worked quietly that day and gained some more support as a future leader. Philip Gayelin of the *Washington Post* argued that his eight hours in power "showed a George Bush both sensible and sensitive enough to carry on business as usual in the absence of any good reason to do otherwise."[70]

Bush returned to his unobtrusive role following Reagan's recovery, but his people were continuing to point toward 1988. Bush began to face attacks from other GOP contenders because of a poll the Republican National Committee was conducting asking people about the strengths and weaknesses of the vice president. Anger arose because the Bush campaign conducted this poll without having to pay for it. The poll did take place without Bush funds, but according to Evans and Novak, Bush was not likely to be pleased with the results. "Bush's relatively low score on leadership, combined with the sentiments among some that he is weak," they wrote, "shows that Bush needs to find opportunities to demonstrate leadership and to develop an image less dependent on his connection to Reagan."[71] This warning came from Robert Teeter, a Bush pollster and strategist. Evans and Novak concluded that "while the vice president needs to maintain the assets and diminish the liabilities of the Reagan connection, he cannot risk the public's trust in him through sharp political practice."[72] Bush was already dealing with the the vice presidential dilemma three years before the election.

At the end of 1985, Bush attempted to appear more aggressive to conservatives. Marlin Fitzwater, Bush's press secretary, announced that the vice president would speak at a dinner honoring the late William Loeb of New Hampshire. Fitzwater stated: "The vice president is a conservative. His voting record in Congress was conservative. His support of the president is both personal and philosophical and we think it appropriate to let everyone know that."[73] The significance of Bush attending the Loeb dinner was the history these two men shared. William Loeb was the powerful editor of the *Manchester Union Leader* who savagely attacked Bush in New Hampshire during his unsuccessful 1980 campaign, and many questioned whether Bush was pandering for conservative support by accepting the invitation to speak. Bush would have to chart a steady course as more candidates emerged in the next year. Bush was the front-runner, but a weak front-runner.

George Bush concentrated on two tasks in 1986. The first was his continuing effort to court the right wing of the Republican party in order to ensure his nomination in 1988. The second was his all-consuming attempt to minimize his involvement in the Iran/Contra scandal that broke in October 1986. This controversy called into question his relationship with Reagan, and it also threatened to destroy his campaign before Bush had officially announced his intentions.

Bush devoted most of the year to efforts to gain the support of Republicans and show some independence. In January, Mark Shields of the *Washington Post* offered his solution for the vice president: "So what George Bush needs most of all is an issue and a cause of his own, something that will establish his independent identity."[74] Shield questioned how effective it was for Bush to speak to conservative audiences in an effort to gain their support. "By continuing his present course of publicly caressing the erogenous zones of the right side of the body politic, Bush will look more and more like a lap dog than an independent leader."[75] Bush was gaining the acceptance of the right wing, but its members never totally embraced him. An endorsement from Reagan would do far more for Bush than speaking at conservative functions.

Other commentators followed Shield's lead. William F. Buckley compared Bush to Hubert Humphrey in 1968 without a major issue, such as Vietnam, directing the campaign. "It will be very difficult for Mr. Bush given this recent history to say in effect that Republicans owe him the nomination because of his standing."[76] Bush discussed what he would say to the people when he ran for president. "Here's what we've done. "Here's what's worked and here's what hasn't. We're moving into a new decade and here's what I think ought to be done."[77] One can easily see in Bush's statement the use of the word "we" in describing the Reagan administration. This closeness to Reagan was Bush's greatest asset and potentially his greatest liability.

Bush received a lot of criticism from the press for his seeming pandering to the right, but apparently his efforts did not hurt him in the polls, which had him with almost a forty-point lead over Senator Howard Baker of Tennessee in May. Bush received advice on running his campaign from Raymond Price, a former speech writer for Richard Nixon, passed on in a column by Philip Gayelin. "He would have the vice president latch on to a few pieces of the Reagan program and make them his own, rally support for them, clobber the opposition and in the process convey where he, George Bush wants to take the country between now and the eve of the 21st century."[78]

Bush formed a committee to raise money and to test the waters in a Michigan straw poll. Some political commentators argued that he would spend almost $750,000 to ensure that he did well. The only politically bad news for Bush that summer was the entry of Paul Laxalt into the race for president. The conservative senator from Nevada was a close friend of Ronald Reagan, and since Bush had not yet received the endorsement of the president, the possibility of Laxalt gaining the nod was a problem. Bush still enjoyed greater name recognition, and the future looked good until October when the Iran/Contra affair became known.

The Iran/Contra scandal had two elements. The first element concerned Iran and American hostages held in Lebanon. In return for selling missiles and spare parts to Iran through Israel, the United States would hopefully gain the release of its hostages. The second element concerned Nicaraguan freedom fighters known as Contras. Any profits gained from selling arms to Iran were sent to fund the contras. This diversion of funds was illegal after Congress decided that the government should halt supplying the contras.

The problem with the Iran/Contra affair for Bush was not the diversion of funds to supply the Contras, but the exchange of missiles for hostages. Bush had been placed in charge of a special task force to combat terrorism, and it was the policy of the administration not to negotiate with terrorists. Bush faced criticism for attending many of the meetings where this plan was adopted without offering any opposition. Bush quickly defended Reagan's actions, and he supported Reagan's somewhat specious contention that it was not an arms-for-hostages deal. Bush also claimed that he was attending the Army-Navy game while a critical meeting about a hostage deal was taking place.

The Iran/Contra affair dominated the news for the next few months. David Broder covered the vice president closely in the press. "Bush's fortunes are obviously tied to how well the administration does, one senior adviser said, and right now it's not doing very well."[79] Bush finally spoke out publicly on the affair. "I understand the skepticism of the American people. Clearly mistakes were made. . . . There can be no denying that our credibility has been damaged. The president has moved strongly and swiftly. We want the truth. The president wants it. I want it. . . . Let's go forward together."[80] Reagan's action was to appoint a commission to investigate the affair chaired by Senator John Tower. Bush said he intended to wait for the commission's report before making any additional comments. Broder wanted more from Bush:

What Bush had done on this occasion, as on others is to tell the truth—but not the whole truth. Out of loyalty, he has stopped short of expressing clearly his own views and feelings or setting forth the record of his own actions. What he has said, I feel for sure is true. What he has not said is crucial.[81]

For Bush, being a good vice president was being a loyal vice president. He often said that "loyalty is not a character flaw."[82] He also made it clear that he did not intend to discuss his role in Iran/Contra further: "I could care less. I've said what I think. If that helps, fine, if it hurts fine, I'm not going to change."[83]

Bush was facing a crossroads as 1987 began. He was ahead in the polls, and he had remained loyal to Ronald Reagan, although a formal endorsement was still lacking. His attitude of being a loyal vice president had encountered some scrutiny, but nothing damaging. With the revelation of Iran/Contra, however, his role as vice president was called into question. Why did Bush not offer opposition to a plan that was against the public policy of the Reagan administration? If he was at the Army-Navy game during a crucial meeting, what does that say about his importance within the Reagan White House? Bush received much advice from aides and columnists to come out with a separate agenda for himself. Iran/Contra made this a difficult task. Bush had to remain closely associated with Reagan but also far enough away so that the scandal did not cause his campaign to collapse. Bush would be balancing on this tightrope for the next two years.

Then, the news for Bush improved. Felix Rodriguez, alias Max Gomez, a supplier for the Contras in Nicaragua, stated that he never discussed his missions with Bush. "I never discussed this involvement with anyone in the vice president's staff until August 8, 1986, as described in the chronology released by the vice president's office."[84] Despite this development, Bush's undeclared candidacy seemed to be grinding to a halt. No longer was he speaking at conservative functions looking for conservative support. Evans and Novak questioned the new attitude of Bush and his advisors in the middle of February. Their column focused on Bush's decision not to attend the annual Conservative Political Action Conference (CPAC) in Washington:

Considering Bush's earlier progress with the religious right and the fact that the conservative movement's loyalty is yet to be won by anyone, Bush's conduct cannot be explained as a hard political strategy. Rather, efforts to stifle criticism from his moderate supporters that he is pandering to the right smack of the premature front-runner attitude that often has characterized his campaign.[85]

Evans and Novak had their own suggestion of strategy for the vice president. "Instead of skipping CPAC and pressuring party chairmen, the vice president at long last might better cut the umbilical cord to the Reagan administration and strike out on his own."[86]

In early March, when Bush returned to the campaign trail in Iowa, he was naturally met by questions about Iran/Contra. Bill Peterson and Edward Walsh covered the vice president's campaign swing for the *Washington Post*. According to their coverage, Bush was pleased with the Tower Report, which concluded that Bush was basically out of the loop regarding decisions made about Iran/Contra. Recent polls in Iowa showed Bush now trailing Robert Dole, and one Iowan asked Bush how he planned to stem the tide. "You hold your head up, you do the best you can, you spell out your vision. . . . Say what you think, tell the truth and do so with a sense of honor," responded Bush.[87] Once again, however, the vice president failed to detail where he was planning to take the nation. He was called to task for it by Richard Cohen of the *Washington Post*.

Cohen argued that Bush should set an agenda for himself or face the disaster that struck Hubert Humphrey in 1968. "Bush forever wants it both ways to be loyal and yet not accountable," he said. "All this follows from Bush's first mistake, which was to accept the vice presidential nomination from a man with whom he disagreed on important matters."[88] Cohen offered an interesting conclusion, stating that "Bush's efforts to remain close to Reagan is both startling and disturbing and it will dog Bush throughout his campaign. He could well lose this time for the same reason he did last time: he cannot stand comparison with Ronald Reagan."[89]

Ever since Bush became a presidential contender, people have compared him with Martin Van Buren, Richard Nixon, and Hubert Humphrey. These comparisons have simply been made because they were all incumbent vice presidents. No one went further until David Broder read Stephen Ambrose's study of Nixon and wrote a column in May comparing Nixon and Bush. Broder argued that Reagan had been far kinder with his vice president than Eisenhower was with Nixon. "Reagan, from all reports, has been far more gracious personally to Bush and permitted no doubt about his desire to keep Bush as his running mate in 1984," he said.[90] Broder also argued that Bush had shown more loyalty to Reagan than Nixon showed to Eisenhower and perhaps that was why Bush was having difficulties with his campaign. "The comparative history of the two men shows why Bush is thought of as even less 'his own man' than Nixon was when he sought the presidency."[91] Bush had to offer a vision or face the same fate as Richard Nixon in 1960.

Bush decided to project a new image in late May. He carefully began to discuss issues such as assistance to college students. At the same time, Bush avoided any criticism of President Reagan. Congressman Jim Leach of Iowa noted what Bush should do in this regard: "He's got to make it clear he's future oriented, that he symbolizes something different than the person in office, but in no sense be perceived as disloyal."[92]

Bush's efforts to come out on his own earned for him the cover and feature story in the June issue of the *National Journal*. Bush commented on his belief that being vice president had affected the perception of his independence: "I took a lot of shots in 1984 running against Congresswoman Ferraro on that account. But I don't think it says anything about character, except something good. Loyalty is strength, a very great strength."[93] Bush made it clear that he would not voice any disagreement with the policies of Ronald Reagan, including Iran/Contra. "The only thing that matters is mutual trust between the President and the Vice President. And if that is missing, you don't get any substantive things to do."[94] The *National Journal* concluded that "his political fortunes, buoyed so far by his loyalty to Reagan, are likely to rise or fall on his ability to convince voters that he is his own man."[95]

Bush had started to chart his own path, but he was still questioned about his knowledge of Iran/Contra. This continued pressure changed the emphasis of Bush's campaign very quickly. Just a month after beginning the process of voicing his ideas about the future, Bush shifted gears and began to focus on his impressive résumé. David Hoffman of the *Washington Post* reported on the about-face: "The vice president's political strategists have frequently said one of his strong suits is a stature advantage over other candidates, referring to his many jobs in government and politics."[96] This change in the Bush campaign's focus did not stop his decline in the polls or attacks by other Republicans.

The major attackers were Robert Dole and Pete DuPont. Dole began to discuss how he was rated higher by independents and Democrats than

Bush. "The national committeemen want a qualified winner, not a qualified loser."[97] Pete DuPont raised questions about the decision of the vice president not to debate the other candidates until he formally announced his candidacy. "George Bush has said his loyalty to President Reagan has prevented him from speaking out on the issues. This silence is no longer a virtue; it is fast becoming a liability for the Republican Party."[98] Bush later decided to join the debate, but the damage was done.

At summer's end, Reagan made a statement that sounded very much like a statement discussed earlier that President Eisenhower had made during the 1960 campaign. Reagan was interviewed in September by *USA Today*, and the *Washington Post* reprinted part of the interview. In the article, Reagan discussed how he liked to delegate authority ever since his days as governor of California:

I had the same resolution when I came here about the vice president. You don't leave that kind of ability out in another room while you're discussing all the decisions to be made. And so he just hasn't been feeling my pulse, sitting by. He has been actively engaged. He's been all over the world in our behalf as an emissary. And not just at funerals—with actual missions.[99]

When Reagan was asked to give an example of a policy or two that the vice president influenced, he replied, "I can't answer in that context."[100] This interview was basically worthless to the vice president as he was about to announce his candidacy.

Bush finally launched his second campaign for the presidency on October 12, 1987, in Houston, Texas. He declared that Americans "don't need radical directions."[101] He argued that "we need strong and steady and experienced leadership."[102] Bush discussed the success of the Reagan administration but not its failures. He failed to discuss any specific issues, but he did repeat his long and impressive résumé and sought to project himself as being more compassionate than many thought. Bush then left Houston for Illinois to accept the endorsement of Governor James Thompson.

In 1987, George Bush was far different from the candidate who declared his candidacy for president eight years earlier. Bush had served one of the nation's most popular presidents for seven years. To come out with a vastly new agenda was virtually impossible. His devout loyalty had weakened him in many eyes, and unanswered questions about Iran/Contra continued to bother him. Ronald Reagan had not anointed him as his successor and had helped to diminish his role in that September interview. But he still needed the president's support if he gained the Republican nomination. Bush had to hope that in the next few months Reagan would not give his support to someone else or have another Iran/Contra stumble, which could make Bush's efforts to hold on to the coattails of Ronald Reagan worthless. In any case, Bush had to fight the fight of his life for the presidency. This was a fight that many columnists argued Bush did not want.

Martin Van Buren was in a far better position in 1835 than George Bush in 1987. Van Buren had already secured his party's nomination and the undying support of Andrew Jackson. Van Buren could focus on the opposition party and its attacks. Bush had to deal with hostile Republicans attacking his importance and then the Democratic Party, which would make its case against the Reagan years. No one could say at these respective points of their campaigns that the elections of Van Buren and Bush were ensured. Many other obstacles and political dangers emerged as both men attempted to follow the large footsteps of Andrew Jackson and Ronald Reagan.

# 3

# Solving the Dilemma

In their respective races for the presidency, neither Martin Van Buren nor George Bush won by a landslide, but they enjoyed comfortable victories over disorganized opponents. Their victories were not certain months prior to the elections. Problems for both men caused some to doubt their ultimate victory. This chapter looks at their respective campaigns and shows how Van Buren and Bush were able to overcome the vice-presidential curse that has haunted other vice presidents with presidential aspirations.

Political problems for Van Buren were prevalent during his campaign. It is extremely difficult to run a campaign against one candidate, let alone three. The Whig party did not unify behind Henry Clay but ran three regional campaigns. Van Buren's managers changed the campaign's focus to White as each contender dropped out. Toward the end of the campaign, Van Buren was aware of possible Whig efforts to bypass the people and throw the election into the House of Representatives. The possibility also remained for an ingenious plot to get a Whig vice presidential candidate from New York elected by the Senate prior to Van Buren's election and make him constitutionally ineligible for the presidency. (If the presidential election was a stalemate, the Whigs that had control of the Senate would select the vice president.)

Van Buren also had to contend with problems from within his campaign. His running mate, Richard Johnson, was not accepted in many areas, especially in Virginia, where the people nominated and supported another candidate in November. No one directly explained the opposition to Johnson, but this study will look at his personal life in an effort to understand the problems. Van Buren also had splinter parties in his home state that could cause him difficulties. Loco Focos and Anti-Masons did not nominate presidential candidates on their own, but their votes could decide the election in close states and possibly aid the Whigs in tossing the election to the House of Representatives.

The Anti Masons opposed the secret society of Masons since the murder of William Morgan in 1828 and nominated William Wirt for president in 1832. (Morgan was a disgruntled ex-Mason who threatened to write a book revealing the secrets of Freemasonry.) The Loco Focos were a radical offshoot of the Democratic party and acquired their unique name when the lights were turned out at one of their meetings, and the members restored the light by igniting their loco foco matches. Throughout this campaign, Van Buren maintained the accepted role of a presidential candidate and did no direct campaigning other than some letter writing. President Jackson and his operatives did more direct campaigning. Just how important was this effort? Was this campaign an effort to elect Van Buren or to vote for the continuation of the Jackson years?

George Bush faced two campaigns during his quest to claim the presidency. His first campaign for the Republican nomination was the effort to get over the hump on Iran/Contra which came to light in the autumn of 1986, and to eliminate the so-called wimp factor, which had plagued Bush since his 1980 run for the presidency. Many believed that Bush was not tough enough to run for president. Following a terrible finish in the Iowa caucuses, Bush was able to save his campaign through a heated interview with television news anchor Dan Rather. Bush emerged as a stronger candidate, and after defeating Bob Dole in the New Hampshire primary, he moved quickly to squash his opposition and gain the nomination. Bush finally received Reagan's endorsement and prepared for the general election campaign against Michael Dukakis.

The general election campaign did not begin well for Bush. Michael Dukakis was an efficient governor from Massachusetts, and until the first debate with Bush, he did very well in the polls. Bush improved his polling numbers throughout the summer, but a potential problem arose with his selection of Senator Dan Quayle from Indiana as his running mate. Quayle did not have the personal problems of Van Buren's Richard Johnson, but his undistinguished political career made him appear to be a lightweight in comparison to Dukakis' running mate Lloyd Bentsen of Texas. Bentsen was the same man who had defeated Bush in his 1970 Senate race. Quayle's low point occurred during the vice presidential debate, where Bentsen outshined him, but in 1988, the public was voting for the top of the ticket and not for the running mate. Political times had certainly changed since Van Buren's time, and it was expected that Bush would actively campaign on his own behalf. His staff's use of negative campaigning and Dukakis' own gaffes helped Bush emerge as the more respected leader. In this case too, we must seek to determine whether the public was voting for a Bush presidency or for a continuation of the Reagan years.

## SUCCEEDING OLD HICKORY

In May 1835, Van Buren emerged from the Democratic convention in Baltimore as the presidential candidate of the party he had helped to create around Andrew Jackson. His efforts had brought him to the brink of the presidency, but as a result of creating a party supporting Jackson, he had helped create the preconditions for a party that opposed Jackson and now posed a threat to his own political aspirations. The Whig party operated its first presidential campaign in 1836 and hoped to defeat the chosen successor of Andrew Jackson.

What was a Whig? President Jackson offered this answer: "A Whig was a man devoid of principle and honesty, a man completely untrustworthy."[1] Putting aside Jackson's prejudices, some men who considered themselves Whigs simply opposed everything Andrew Jackson stood for. Other Whigs were avid supporters of Henry Clay and his American System. Another faction of the Whig party included strong sectionalists and followers of John C. Calhoun. Victory was possible for the new party if it could unify behind one candidate and offer one message. The Whig party did not hold a nominating convention but relied on state legislature and caucuses to nominate its candidates. The diverse elements that called themselves Whigs were only united in their goal to replace the Democrats. The Whig party found itself running a sectional campaign for president in 1836 with the hope of defeating Van Buren at the polls or in the House of Representatives. The three candidates the Whigs settled on were Daniel Webster in the North, Hugh White in the South, and William Henry Harrison in the West. Each candidate offered something for the voter, but none of the three was strong enough on his own.

### Daniel Webster

At the outset of the campaign, Webster was by far the best known of the candidates opposing Van Buren. The popular senator from Massachusetts had helped to organize the Whig party along with Henry Clay and was expected to be the strongest challenger to Van Buren.

Following the Democratic convention, Whig supporters gathered together in Massachusetts to nominate a candidate. They naturally selected their favorite son, Senator Daniel Webster. The Whig rally met in Faneuil Hall in Boston on May 28, 1835, and unanimously endorsed Webster for president. In late June, the Massachusetts legislature made it official and formally nominated Webster. The new candidate immediately realized that he needed to run a national campaign if he had any hope of defeating Van

Buren. He saw Ohio and the Midwest as pivotal regions and hoped that he could persuade William Henry Harrison to be his running mate.

Webster wrote to his good friend Edward Everett on July 2, 1835, and made this suggestion about Harrison and the fourth of July: "It would be very well if on the Fourth in various places General Harrison should be toasted as Whig Candidate for the vice presidency."[2] Webster's plan failed to draw Harrison to him, since the general had already been bitten by the presidential bug. Webster continued his campaign for the presidency, but he was not prepared for campaigning in a period of increasing voter participation with the end of or reduction of property requirements to vote.

Late in February 1836, Webster suggested to his supporters in Massachusetts that he wished to withdraw his candidacy. "Indeed in the state of things at present existing in the country," he said, "my personal wishes are to withdraw my name from the place it occupies before the public in connection with the approaching election."[3] Massachusetts quickly reaffirmed its support for Webster, but for all intents and purposes, his campaign for the presidency was over.

### Hugh White

Hugh White campaigned to the end against Van Buren. From the political insiders of the day, White's campaign was one based on the ideas from which Jackson was elected on in 1828. White was a friend of Andrew Jackson and had been offered the cabinet post of Secretary of War in 1828 and 1831. White broke with Jackson over his decision to seek another term in 1832 and over the choice of Van Buren as his running mate in 1832 and heir apparent in 1836. White refused to attend the 1832 Democratic convention in Baltimore and gave this explanation: "I am for Gen. Jackson; but am not either a Calhoun Jackson man, or a Van Buren Jackson man."[4] White campaigned for Jackson, but he did not want to be involved in the questions of succession. "I will go on exactly as I have done, making myself as useful as I can; determined to leave myself at liberty, when Gen. Jackson is off the stage, to exercise my own judgment on the question of succession."[5]

Other Jackson supporters shared White's feelings about the president selecting his successor. Had Tennessee allowed a delegation to attend the Baltimore Convention in May 1835, it would have supported White over Van Buren. White's supporters decided to use the same vehicle that Jackson had used in 1825—legislative nomination. The Tennessee legislature nominated White on October 17, 1835, and offered its opinions about the convention that had just nominated Van Buren for president:

In the organization and proceedings of the late Baltimore Convention we perceive the same violation of the spirit of the Constitution, the same tendency to an usurpation of the rights and powers of the people in the election of a president, the same spirit of intrigue, the same liability in the members to be corrupted and influenced in their course by the promise and expectation of office, which we saw in the organization and proceedings of the Congressional caucus in 1823, and then condemned in the most public and solemn manner.[6]

White portrayed himself as following the traditional beliefs by which Jackson operated during his first term in office. Van Buren operatives tried to show White's disloyalty to Jackson throughout the campaign in many newspaper articles and brand him as a Whig. White denied these allegations and was more determined to remain in the race. White believed that he was the only candidate espousing true democratic principles. The Whig party viewed White as a useful tool in blocking the election of Van Buren and did not refute the charges of White being a Whig.

White posed a great challenge to Van Buren in Tennessee and throughout the South. White's efforts were assisted by Davy Crockett, a former Tennessee congressman and author of an unauthorized biography of Van Buren.

White's campaign had a national focus from the start, including a proposed large printing of Crockett's biography on Van Buren. But as the campaign continued, White's candidacy became relegated to the South and then eventually to just Tennessee. White did not enjoy Van Buren's name recognition nor the military heroics of Harrison. White also faced the full force of Jackson supporters in Tennessee, including the president. For White's campaign to succeed, Van Buren had to stumble on an issue of particular interest to the South. Slavery was this issue and Van Buren had to face it in order to capture the presidency in 1836.

### William Henry Harrison

The final candidate to oppose Van Buren began as the greatest longshot and ended up being the strongest challenger to Jackson's heir apparent. William Henry Harrison relied on his military fame during the War of 1812 and not on his political experience to carry him to the White House. Running as a military hero from humble log cabin origins proved successful for Harrison in 1840, but in 1836, the organization of the Whig party was not complete.

Harrison was a member of a respected family and had served in the military for almost thirty years. Harrison also was territorial governor of Indiana and had served two terms in Congress. He was viewed as a supporter of Henry Clay and had hoped without success to be his running mate in 1832. Harrison was nominated in January 1835 by Hamilton County in Ohio. Harrison did far more active campaigning than the other candidates with much attention focused on his war record during the War of 1812.

Harrison spent the years before the war fighting various Indian tribes in the Midwest. He fought bravely at the Battle of Tippecanoe against the Shawnee but failed to achieve a lasting peace. The battle did earn him the nickname Old Tippecanoe. During the War of 1812, his claim to fame was his victory at the Battle of Thames, where the great Shawnee chief Tecumseh was killed. Harrison and his forces were saved that day by troops under the command of Richard Johnson, and in 1836, Harrison had to share some of the credit with Van Buren's running mate.

In his public life, Harrison had the misfortune to support measures that later would make him look foolish during the 1836 presidential campaign. One example was his support of legislation that placed whites in slavery for debt. The legislation failed to pass, but Harrison's support of this measure made most of the newspapers. Harrison also had to show during the campaign that at sixty-three, he was not old or senile. He did this by going on extended tours of the West and the North. He was so well received on his first tour that he refused to consider becoming Daniel Webster's running mate.

In June 1835, Harrison received the endorsement of the Virginia Whigs, which was printed in the *Richmond Enquirer*:

Resolved therefore that we view General William Henry Harrison as the candidate of the people, and give our decided preference over any individual now in nomination for President of the United States, first, because we have the fullest confidence in his talents, great moral worth, political principles, strict integrity and civil qualifications; secondly, because of his long and meritorious service, both in the field and in the councils of the Nation, which justly entitle him to a large share of National honor.[7]

Harrison continued his extensive campaigning in 1835 and 1836 and ultimately replaced Webster as the candidate of the North and outshined White in the border states and the Southwest.

### The Campaign Biography

Each candidate sponsored the writing of a campaign biography about him. In Van Buren's case, he was also the subject of an unauthorized biography by Davy Crockett. Crockett wanted Hugh White to be elected president in 1836. In a little over 200 pages, Crockett discussed Van Buren's entire life and why one should support Hugh White as the legitimate successor to Andrew Jackson. Crockett got this book published after he realized that his own presidential ambitions would not be successful in 1836. Crockett's name is the only author listed because the publishers feared libel suits from Van Buren. (This biography will be studied briefly.) His book hurt Van Buren especially in the South, but it lost most of its sting after Crockett's death at the Alamo in March 1836. Crockett's book then was just used to attack Van Buren in White's home state of Tennessee.

Crockett described in detail Van Buren's actions that garnered Jackson's sponsorship. He focused primarily on Van Buren's slyness and on the illegitimacy of Van Buren's appointment as heir apparent:

If you ask them [the supporters of Van Buren] what it is that makes Van Buren fit for a president, and why it is that General Jackson has appointed him for his successor, they answer, he has been persecuted for Jackson's sake. Jackson, they say, has done enough, not only to rein himself as long as he wants to, but to say who shall rein after him. But the good of this joke is, these same people call themselves democratic republicans: Republicans! Unable to choose for themselves, and continuing to give that right to a single individual. What think you of that?[8]

Crockett had been a supporter of Jackson's, but he now questioned whether Jackson was being manipulated by the men around Van Buren:

I say, then, it is in vain to deny that if Van Buren is elected, it is wholly and solely upon the strength of General Jackson's popularity, and his having the good fortune to be selected by the old gentlemen as his successor. He nor his friends plead no merit in himself; there is not manner of good thing in him, and that he has no earthly chance of reaching the presidential chair but in and through the greatest and best.[9]

From reading Crockett, it seems that many of Van Buren's detractors would have voted for another term of Old Hickory if he was not under the influence of the "magician." Despite his disgust for Van Buren, Crockett still had a great deal of respect for Jackson. "Jackson is open, bold, warm hearted, confiding, and passionate to a fault," he wrote. "Van Buren is secret, sly, selfish, cold, calculating, distrustful, treacherous; and if he could gain an object just as well by openness as intrigue, he would choose the latter."[10]

Crockett then went on to discuss Van Buren's entire political career. He focused on the early criticism of Van Buren as noncommittal on many issues. "Van Buren is found first on one side and then on the other; and not content, as most people would be, with showing their dexterity once, he has crossed over like the mazes of a country dance, not merely once, but twice or thrice in the same figure."[11]

Crockett discussed how Van Buren switched allegiance to Jackson after the failed William Crawford campaign in 1824. Crockett viewed Calhoun as Jackson's heir apparent in 1828 and Van Buren as usurping that position. Crockett blamed Van Buren for allowing Crawford's explanation of the 1818 debate in Monroe's cabinet regarding Jackson's military conduct to damage Calhoun's relationship with the president. He also argued that Van Buren encouraged Crawford to come forward and write to Jackson about the incident. Van Buren was also blamed for keeping the Eaton affair going and using this problem to win the confidence of Jackson and to break up the cabinet and force out supporters of Calhoun, diminishing his influence with Jackson.

Crockett admitted that Van Buren was extremely lucky in being rejected as minister to England:

It put the finishing stroke to those plans so artfully laid, and which I have so fully explained, to bring over General Jackson and his powerful popularity exclusively to his interest so settled and fixed as to prevent its withdrawal even in favour of the longest and best friend he ever had in his life. General Jackson considered it an insult to himself, and from that moment he identified himself with Van Buren; and the consequences which followed show what one unfortunate step will sometimes do.[12]

Crockett's goal in preparing this biography was to promote the candidacy of Hugh White. He spent considerable time comparing the two men and criticizing Jackson and others for telling the people for whom they should vote. Crockett portrayed White as a man of the people who had fought alongside Jackson during the War of 1812, while Van Buren was safe in New York. "While White was fighting the Indians, who were murdering the women and children on the frontiers, and laying their habitations in ashes, Van Buren was snugly and safely standing up in the Senate of New York, branding the war as unjust, unnecessary and unwise."[13]

Crockett also discussed the so-called abuse of Van Buren over the years, which had been documented by the *Argus* and other newspapers and discussed by Senator Thomas Hart Benton of Missouri and Thomas Ritchie, the editor of the *Richmond Enquirer*:

Mr. Benton and Tom Ritchie are trying to persuade the people that Mr. Van Buren has been more abused than any man in America, except Mr. Jefferson; and they expect Mr. Jefferson merely for the benefit of comparing Van Buren to that great man, thinking the people will take it for granted that as Mr. Jefferson was made president because he was so much abused, Mr. Van Buren ought to be also, for the same reason.[14]

In its literature, the Whig party gave a great deal of attention to what they considered as Jackson's abuse of presidential power. The disgust over Jackson's selection of Van Buren as his successor was a prominent feature of the White campaign. Following Crockett's death, White continued to voice his outrage over Van Buren's selection as a presidential candidate in the first place. It seems that all White supporters shared the conclusion of Davy Crockett:

There is one thing in which I think all will agree, that Martin Van Buren is not the man he is cracked up to be and that if he is made president of the United States, he will have reached a place to which he is not entitled, either by sense or sincerity; and that he owes his good luck to the hangers-on of office, who, to serve themselves, have used the popularity of General Jackson to abuse the country with Martin Van Buren.[15]

## The Campaign

The general election campaign began for Van Buren after his nomination in May 1835. He had no problem securing an unanimous nomination, but his running mate Richard Johnson faced serious opposition. Richard Mentor Johnson was born in Floyd's Station, Kentucky, on October 17, 1780. Johnson had military aptitude and became a hero during The War of 1812 at the Battle of the Thames in 1813. Johnson received many wounds and was credited with being the man who killed the great Shawnee Chief Tecumseh. After the war, Johnson served Kentucky as a congressman and then a senator who worked for a seven-day postal service, the end of imprisonment for debt, and for an increase in congressional salaries. The problem for the gentleman known for always wearing a red vest and ready to show one his war wounds was his personal life, which disgusted many and worried many others. What was wrong then with the senator from Kentucky?

The Senate doorkeeper referred to Johnson as being "the most vulgar man of all vulgar men in this world."[16] Even James K. Polk, an important Van Buren supporter in Tennessee and throughout the South, argued that "Johnson would be a deadweight on the Democratic ticket there."[17]

As a young man Johnson had fallen in love with a woman, but his mother disapproved because his bride-to-be was a working girl. Following his father's death, Johnson inherited the family slaves and took one, named Julia Chin, as his companion. Johnson enjoyed many years with Julia and had two daughters with her. When his daughters became teenagers, Johnson tried to present them to the public unsuccessfully. Johnson received more criticism for his actions following Julia's death in 1833.

Johnson took another companion from his slaves who ran off. He finally caught up with her and then sold her at a slave auction. Johnson then returned home and took her sister as his new companion. People who knew of Johnson's activities did not publicly discuss his relationship with Julia and the other women. Detractors argued that Johnson was not morally fit to be vice president. Attacks on Johnson continued throughout the campaign. It appears that Johnson did love Julia and their children. His actions after her death, however, seemed to be the actions of a slave owner who is using his position for sexual favors. Historians and those involved at the time argue that Johnson may have hurt Van Buren in the South, but was a help to him in the West.

Many people remembered that Johnson was a war hero whose crippled hand was a constant reminder of his exploits. A representative from Kentucky offered this defense of Johnson at the Democratic convention following the demonstration against him by Virginia and other delegations:

With daring impetuosity, he pursued and overtook the enemy—threw himself like a Thunderbolt of war into the thicket of the fight—fought hand to hand and eye to eye with the Briton, and his savage myrmidons—poured out his blood like water—triumphed and returned, loaded with the richest trophies of the campaign. Sir, his life has been one the unfaltering, unanswering devotions to freedom and to the people.[18]

Virginia refused to support Johnson and placed in nomination William Rives at the convention. During the campaign, Virginia supported William Smith of Alabama for the vice presidency. The Virginia delegation believed that Johnson would hurt the party, even though Johnson had significant support from the general public. Representative Joseph Holt of Kentucky argued that Virginia was wrong:

They have nothing to fear for the fate of their nominence; he is fortressed behind principles and popular attachments, impregnable as Gibraltar. The people have twined the wreath of glory around his brow—the harpy hand of faction cannot tear it off, nor can the sirocco breath of a myriad of calumniators wither the eternal freshness of its emerald.[19]

The *Albany Argus* was generally pleased with the ticket of Van Buren and Johnson, even with the controversy over Van Buren's running mate. Henry Clay quickly made his opinion known to his political confidant John Cobaris on the upcoming election. "Independent of other objections to Mr. Van Buren, it would be perfectly decisive against him with me, that he is sought to be forced upon the People by General Jackson."[20] Many still believed that eventually Clay would emerge to take on Van Buren.

In the middle of June, the *Argus* printed Van Buren's formal acceptance of the Democratic party's nomination. Van Buren accepted the nomination and responded to his possible succession of Jackson and following in Old Hickory's footsteps:

I have neither solicited the aid nor sought the support of any man in reference to the high office for which I have been nominated; unless my replies to interrogatories from my fellow citizens upon public questions and my sincere endeavors to make myself worthy of the respect and confidence of the American people, are liable to that construction.[21]

Van Buren pledged, "I shall if honored by the choice of the American people, endeavor to tread generally in the footsteps of President Jackson—happy if I shall be able to perfect the work he has so gloriously begun."[22] In his acceptance letter, Van Buren did not offer his positions on the issues of the day. He indicated he would be willing to respond to letters requesting his opinions.

The nomination of Daniel Webster by the Massachusetts legislature quickly followed by the end of June. Henry Clay had doubts whether Webster or White could defeat Van Buren in 1836.

There is a positive hatred of Mr. Van Buren, and no attachment to Judge White. Mr. Webster does not take. The people appear to be disposed to admire him, but not to vote for him. I am sorry for it; for I should greatly prefer him to either of the other two. I should regard the election of Mr. Van Buren as a great calamity; Judge White's not quite so great.[23]

The *Argus* spent the rest of the summer attacking the Whig party on its efforts to find a candidate to beat Van Buren. The opposition was also criticized for calling themselves other names than Whig in an effort to gain supporters. Webster supporters were beginning to call the party the American party or Constitutional party. Webster was also charged with being a former Federalist. At this point, the *Argus* reprinted an article from the *Washington Globe* on the so-called American party:

In the same way the same party have degraded a succession of appellation. Federal Republican—National Republican—American System—and finally the old revolutionary watchword Whig. This system is now carried a step further. Mr. Webster, the real head of the old monarchical party, is now to be completely identified with the charter of our liberties—and in this way it will be impossible to support the constitution without supporting Mr. Webster.[24]

William Henry Harrison was the busiest candidate during the summer of 1835. He traveled to more than a half dozen states, refusing to become a vice presidential candidate and showing that he was still a vigorous man of sixty-five. The few attacks leveled against him focused on his age and his inability to gain elective office in Ohio, but he was virtually ignored by the Van Buren press. Most attacks continued to be waged against Webster for trying to convince people to forget his past and against White for breaking his ties with Jackson.

As was mentioned briefly, Webster's campaign was not going very well. In November, the beleaguered candidate tried to display a strong difference between himself and Van Buren. In Webster's well-publicized speech, he focused on Van Buren's noncommittalism and his own determination to help America:

I am committed against the derogation from the constitutional authority of congress, and especially against all extension of executive power; and I am committed against any attempt to rule the free people of this country by the power and the patronage of the government itself. I am committed fully and entirely committed against making the government the People's master.[25]

In the same article, the *Argus* defended Van Buren as being a far more principled man, while it analyzed Webster's political career to show how many times he had changed his views on many issues over the years. Webster's speech did not bring new life to his campaign. His quest for the presidency came to a virtual halt causing his withdrawal from active campaigning in early 1836.

The *Argus* printed attacks on Harrison accusing him of being a Federalist and a military failure at the battles of Tippecanoe and Thames. Very early on, the *Argus* discussed the possibility that the ultimate goal of the Whig party in 1836 was to have the presidential election decided in the House of Representatives. President Jackson raised this concern in his annual message to Congress in December 1835:

Every election by the House of Representatives is calculated to lessen the force of that security which is derived from the distinct and separate character of the Legislative and Executive functions, and while it exposes each to temptations adverse to their efficiency as organs of the constitution and laws, its tendency will be to untie both in resisting the will of the People, and thus give a direction to the Government, anti-republican and dangerous.[26]

Van Buren continued to receive praise in some circles as the only candidate capable of following in Andrew Jackson's footsteps. This resolution from the Alabama legislature offers a good example of such support:

We consider him an upright and honorable man, an able statesman, a genuine democrat of the Jefferson school, and a true patriot and lover of his country; that he is at this time, withal, the strong man of the democratic republican party throughout the United States, and standing pledged as he does to carry out the principles which have distinguished the administration of the present Chief Magistrate.[27]

As 1835 drew to a close, the *Argus* printed a story from Kentucky that discussed the possibility that Clay might still enter the race. "Our opinion has always been that Mr. Clay is the only individual upon whom, throughout the Union, we can rally, so as to conquer the Magician and his host of office holders, and, as yet, we have seen nothing in the signs of the times to change that opinion."[28] The new year looked promising for Van Buren, but he still had to face abuse about his running mate and offer his views on the explosive issue of slavery.

Hugh White faced difficulties in early January finding a running mate. P. P. Barbour of Georgia refused to accept a vice presidential nomination. He claimed that he supported White but that his followers were not loyal to the principles that Jackson brought to the presidency in 1828: "I could never consent to place myself in an attitude which would be in direct conflict with an immense majority of the political party, whose principles I have professed and in whose ranks I have stood, since my first entrance on the theater of public life to act my part."[29]

The beginning of 1836 also brought difficulties for Van Buren's running mate in Virginia. The state legislature nominated Van Buren and William Smith of Alabama. Johnson took this slight well and wrote a response to Virginia's actions:

I wish it distinctly understood that so far from making any complaints, by feeling that I had a right or good cause to complain, no man holds more sacredly than I do, the right of the people to make the selection of those in whom they have most confidence; and however honored or flattered I might have considered myself, by the vote of my native state, Virginia. I feel much higher gratification in my exclusion, unless I had been the unbiased choice of a majority of my fellow citizens.[30]

An intriguing aspect of the 1836 campaign was that every candidate for president and vice president, except for William Henry Harrison, held office in the House of Representatives or the Senate and had many encounters with each other. Former vice president, now senator, John C. Calhoun attacked Van Buren in a Senate speech with the vice president in the chair. "He is not (Van Buren) as remarked by Willie P. Magnum, of the race of the lion or the tiger; he belonged to a lower order—the fox and it would be in vain to expect that he could command the respect or acquire the confidence of those who had so little admiration for the qualities by which he was distinguished."[31] Van Buren remained calm, as he would throughout the campaign, and allowed others to defend him.

Friends of Van Buren in Massachusetts gathered in late February at Faneuil Hall to nominate him for president. (Various groups nominated presidential candidates in 1836.) At the same time, Whig publications suggested that Webster should throw his support to Harrison. The *Argus* faced criticism for its comments against Harrison, claiming that the old soldier was poor and was running for president for financial reasons. The *Argus* quickly clarified its position on Harrison: "We have said that his occupancy of the clerkship of Hamilton, the station to which the people of Ohio have deemed it consistent with his merits and qualifications to elevate him, was one of the proofs that the state in which he resides, would not think of him as the recipient of its electoral vote for the presidency."[32]

Van Buren did some campaigning of his own by allowing his opinions on slavery to be published. His response to letters from Virginia and North

Carolina on the power of Congress regarding slavery and especially its status in the District of Columbia were widely circulated. "The relation of master and slave is a matter exclusively belonging to the people of each state, within its own boundary."[33] Van Buren continued, offering his constitutional opinion on this subject: "Thus viewing the matter, I would not, from the lights now before me, feel myself in pronouncing that Congress does not possess the power of interfering with or abolishing slavery in the District of Columbia."[34] Van Buren admitted that Congress had the right to act on the issue of slavery, but he offered his thoughts against action:

I do not hesitate to give to you as my deliberate and well considered opinion, that there are objectors to the exercise of this power, against the wishes of the slave holding States, as imperative in their nature and obligations in regulating the conduct of public men, as the most palpable want of constitutional power would be.[35]

Van Buren's conclusion brought relief to many who believed that he might possibly be an abolitionist:

I do therefore, believe, that the abolition of slavery in the District of Columbia, against the wishes of the slave holding states (assuming that Congress has the power to effect it) would violate the spirit of that compromise of interests which lies at the basis of our social compact; and I am thoroughly convinced that it could not be so done, without imminent peril, if not certain destruction to the Union of the States.[36]

The *Richmond Enquirer* and the *Argus* praised Van Buren for his opinions on this volatile issue, but opinions differed on the effectiveness of Van Buren's letter in the South.

Whig opponents claimed that "the declaration of Mr. Van Buren, that Congress has the right to abolish slavery in the District of Columbia, is completely destroying him in the southern states."[37] This statement might have been true in areas where Van Buren's complete reply was not published, such as North Carolina, but a supporter of Van Buren in Washington claimed the following: "Mr. Van Buren's letter about abolition has completely prostrated the southern panic makers here, who have so long been acting in concert with northern abolitionists. It is a most happy, well timed, and omnipotent paper."[38]

The debate over slavery and Van Buren continued. In April, the *Argus* argued that Van Buren would do a far better job restraining abolitionists than Hugh White:

Mr. Van Buren has wielded in his own state, and if elected president, will undoubtedly be able to wield throughout the north, the greatest influence against that fanatical spirit which would unsettle the compromises of the constitution, and give birth to new political conflicts arising out of domestic relations existing in a portion of the states. Would Judge White be able to exert any power in the north upon the subject? Or would the favorite of the abolitionists at his own door, as well as beyond the borders of his state, be likely to exert such influence if he had it?[39]

Besides slavery, Van Buren had to contend with an issue from his past: the accusation that he was a Catholic. Anti-Catholic rhetoric was common in the United States. This issue was brought up again when Jackson nominated Roger B. Taney to replace John Marshall as Chief Justice of the Supreme Court in March 1836. The *Argus* printed the following allegation:

Roger B. Taney—It will be seen that this man, a Roman Catholic has been appointed and confirmed by the Senate, the successor of John Marshall as Chief Justice of the United States—No doubt Martin Van Buren, the correspondent and eulogist of the Pope, has been active in bringing about this result.[40]

The reference to the Pope referred to a letter Van Buren sent to the Pope while he was secretary of state in 1830. This allegation was repudiated in April by a Mr. Vanderpool, a longtime resident of Kinderhook, New York, who discussed Van Buren's legal support of the Dutch Reformed Church. Van Buren was cleared of any attachment to Catholicism.

Another long-term allegation against Van Buren was the charge that Andrew Jackson was directing his election. John C. Calhoun was just one of those who was very critical of Jackson's influence on the election. "Already has the present Chief Magistrate, at the head of the party, nominated through a mock Convention his successor, and entered personally into the canvass with all the power and influence, which the vast patronage of the Government and the almost unlimited control over the public treasury, with its millions of surplus, give him."[41]

In May, the *Argus* again looked at the possibility that the Whig party wanted to have the election decided in the House of Representatives. This plot started to take greater shape when joint tickets were formed in some states, and in other states, the candidates had the same vice presidential candidate. "If the artifices of the opposition prevail in bringing the election to the House, they must there encounter new obstacles which can only be vanquished by perpetrating a succession of enormities against the rights of the people."[42] The *Argus* failed, however, to explain which candidate the Whigs would support in the House election. The Whig party had failed to support one candidate in the first place. Why would this party made up of so many diverse elements suddenly find common ground to elect a president in the House?

Early in the summer, Van Buren had to face a trap laid by Calhoun in the Senate. Calhoun hoped to force Van Buren into supporting a bill that would hurt his campaign. The bill in question was a measure preventing incendiary publications from being distributed in the South. Van Buren voted for a third reading of the bill and possibly weakened some of his support in the North. Following Van Buren's vote, Webster and other senators came forward and defeated the bill when it came to a final vote. The South could not blame Van Buren and the North could be sent to read his earlier statements on the possibility of ending slavery and causing the destruction of the Union.

After Congress adjourned, President Jackson returned home to Tennessee. Van Buren's supporters stated that Jackson was just making his usual visit home for health reasons. The Whigs had another opinion, which was printed by the *Argus*: "General Jackson is about to make an electioneering tour to the west: This attempt to bring the executive influence to bear on the freedom of elections, will not succeed."[43] Jackson did speak on Van Buren's behalf; his health was, indeed, not good, which was why he returned home.

In July, the focus of the *Argus* turned from attacks on White to Harrison. The impetus for this change was the decision of Virginia's Whigs to cast their lot with Harrison. "Every southern man must feel in General Harrison a confidence of safety on the great question of slavery, which it is impossible he can feel in Van Buren, an avowed distinct abolitionist."[44] The *Argus* followed with its own opinion on Harrison:

For ourselves, we have not deemed the claims or chances of the "Hero of the North Bend" sufficiently formidable to require more than the passing remark, that although doubtless a worthy man, qualified possibly for the duties of the Hamilton county clerkship, he has not been suspected of any serious pretentions to be Presidency of the United States, or any great probability of reaching that station.[45]

While Jackson was still in Tennessee, Hugh White once again spoke out on the president campaigning for Van Buren. "I disagree with this whole doctrine, and insist, it is no part of his duty to select his successor, to have him recommended by a convention, or to use his influence or patronage to induce or coerce persons to vote for him."[46] Even these complaints from White did not disturb Van Buren whose election seemed to some already in the bag. The *Argus* predicted the outcome for every state and gave Van Buren two hundred and seventeen votes to just seventy-seven for his three opponents.

The only bad news for Van Buren was the attitude of the Loco Focos in New York. This radical offshoot of the Democratic party submitted a list of questions to the Democratic ticket. Members received responses from both Van Buren and Johnson. The general committee of Loco Focos was positive in reference to Johnson's response, but not so to Van Buren's. "It is evasive, unsatisfactory, and unworthy of a great statesman. The world, however, will judge of the motive which dictated it."[47] Van Buren, however, did not have much to fear from the Loco Focos or from the Anti-masonic party in 1836. Both parties failed to unite behind a candidate and thus were unable to take many votes away from Van Buren and give them to the opposition.

Van Buren continued to acquire endorsements from powerful figures even after their deaths. Former President James Madison died in the spring of 1836. Before his death, Madison met with the historian and cabinet member George Bancroft to whom he stated his support for Van Buren. In August, Bancroft discussed his meeting with Madison publicly. "The party that rallies around Mr. Van Buren was to Mr. Madison the Party of Union."[48] Van Buren remained the focus of attacks, but they now became more personal. He was criticized for his attire and the style of his coach, but they had little effect on the campaign. Van Buren did write a letter that took up over three pages in the newspaper discussing his positions on the issues. They differed very little with the opinions of the president on distributing revenue surpluses and preventing a new national bank from emerging.

In September, the *Argus* discussed how it now appeared that Harrison was now the Whig candidate of the North and not Daniel Webster. With renewed focus on Harrison, his past record was placed under increased scrutiny. Apparently in 1820, Harrison supported a bill that would enslave whites for debts. The *Argus* came to this conclusion on the Hero of North Bend:

We have hitherto pitied rather blamed him—his want of talent is not his fault; his nomination for the Presidency is not his fault, but that of his friends and his party, and we desired to treat as tenderly as possible the feeble and harmless old man, for such we considered him, till the election should be over, when we would return to the oblivion from which he has been so cruelly dragged.[49]

Van Buren received this glowing remark from President Jackson in early October. "I can say to you that the political horizon is bright and cheering."[50]

As the final months of the campaign moved by, Van Buren was favorably compared to his chief rivals, Harrison and White, by the *Argus*, which attacked White for speaking on the stump in support of his candidacy:

Under the plea of defending himself from the aspersions of our venerable and esteemed "Chief Magistrate," as he more than once jesuitically called Gen. Jackson, he ventured out in the real stump orator style to the great edification of his wondering auditory, and no doubt in his own estimation to the utter discomfiture of those who have been so perverse as not to acknowledge his preeminent claims to the first office in the country.[51]

The *Argus*'s attacks on Harrison were of a more personal nature with references to his age and lack of political experience:

And this is the candidate who is pitted against Mr. Van Buren, by politicians who accuse the latter of non commitalism. We shall not descend to a general comparison of the character and claims of these two candidates. So immeasurably superior is Mr. Van Buren in every statesman like quality, that we shall not question the patriotism and discrimination of the American people so far as to consider any such comparison necessary for a moment.[52]

As the voting began across the nation, which would take almost a month, the possibility of the election being decided in the House of Representatives was once again the subject of an *Argus* article. Late in October, the ingenious plot discussed would make Van Buren ineligible constitutionally for the presidency. The plot would work in this way. If no candidate had a majority of electoral votes, the presidency would then be decided by the House and the vice presidency by the Senate. This plan would have the Whigs keep the House voting deadlocked until the Senate selected Francis Granger of New York as vice president. In the Constitution, the president and the vice president cannot be from the same state. Van Buren would then be left out of the House voting, and the president would be either Harrison or White.

The *Argus*'s final election forecast gave Van Buren two hundred and three electoral votes to eighty-eight for his competitors. As the returns slowly became known in some states, the results looked good for Van Buren. Even Richard Johnson was receiving positive press. In early November, the *Argus* printed a statement made by Harrison about Johnson's role at the Battle of Thames. "It would be useless after stating the circumstances of the action to pass encomiums on Colonel Johnson and his regiment. Veterans could not have manifested more firmness. The Colonel's numerous wounds prove that he was in the post of danger."[53] Johnson also did well when he was compared to New York Congressman Francis Granger in the *Argus*.

Van Buren left New York for Washington on November 14, and it appeared that his election was a certainty. Van Buren was making gains in the North compared to Jackson's efforts in 1832, but he was losing support in the South, including Tennessee, which went for White. By November 23, Van Buren was just three electoral votes short of a majority. Finally the returns from Arkansas and Michigan came in, securing Van Buren's victory. Van Buren received 170 electoral votes to 124 for his rivals. In actual votes cast, Van Buren only defeated the Whigs by a little more than 25,000. Richard Johnson was not elected by the people. Virginia followed its convictions and refused to vote for Johnson, which left him short of a majority. The Senate would select either Francis Granger or Richard Johnson as vice president.

The *Argus* printed attacks made against Johnson prior to the Senate selection:

Colonel Johnson has passed through one ordeal. The people have declared against him. They have rebuked the attempt to confound the distinctions of blood—to violate the laws of nature—to disrupt the foundations of society. Their verdict was rendered, through their elections, against negro amalgamation. It remains for the Senate of the Union to affirm or reverse the decision of the people.[54]

The *Argus* failed to explain that the Senate had no option but to select Johnson. Francis Granger was from New York and was not constitutionally eligible to become vice president. The Senate selected Johnson in February, although senators Calhoun and White walked out rather than vote, and Virginia voted for Granger.

In the months leading up to the inaugural, the Whigs argued that Van Buren was a minority president because of his slim victory and did not have a mandate from the American people. The counterargument was that Van Buren had received more votes for president than any other candidate in history. This, however, was not accurate, since Jackson had defeated Henry Clay in 1832 by more than 150,000 votes. Van Buren's party had lost a lot of support in just four years. The *Argus* stated in January: "They will now judge the administration by its merits and let the Whigs abuse him as much as they please, the country will not permit him to be condemned before he is even tried."[55]

At the end of January, Van Buren bade farewell to the Senate:

Indulging an ardent wish that every success may await you in performing the exalted and honorable duties of your public trust, and offering my warmest prayers that prosperity and happiness may be constant attendents upon each of you along the future paths of life, I respectfully bid you farewell.[56]

The inauguration took place on Saturday, March 4, 1837. The day was a special one for Andrew Jackson and Martin Van Buren. Old Hickory succeeded in getting his final wish. The man taking over the presidency was his personal choice. Van Buren's election indicated that the public desired that the principles and politics he brought to Washington in 1829 be continued.

In Van Buren's speech at the inauguration, he personally thanked Jackson for his service to the nation and his support over the years:

In receiving from the people the sacred trust twice confided to my illustrious predecessor, and which he has discharged so faithfully and so well, I know that I cannot expect to perform the arduous task with equal ability and success. But, united as I have been in his councils, a daily witness of his exclusive and unsurpassed devotion to his country's welfare, agreeing with him in sentiments which his countrymen have warmly supported, and permitted to partake largely of his confidence, I may hope that somewhat of the same cheering approbation will be found to attend upon my path. For him, I but express with my own, the wishes of all—that he may yet long live to enjoy the brilliant evening of his well spent life, and for myself, conscious of but one desire, faithfully to serve my country. I throw myself, without fear, on its justice and its kindness. Beyond that, I only look to the gracious protection of the Divine being, whose strengthening support I humbly solicit, and whom I fervently pray to look down upon us all. May it be among the dispensations of his providence to bless our beloved country with honors and with length of days; may her ways be ways of pleasantness, all her paths be peace.[57]

Thomas Hart Benton summed up the day for many people. "For once the rising was eclipsed by the setting sun."[58] Andrew Jackson left for Tennessee the following week and during the month that it took him to get home, he was greeted with parades, barbeques, and celebrations, thanking him for his years of service. Martin Van Buren was now president of the United States, responsible for running a country that expected a continuation of Old Hickory's policies. Almost at once, Van Buren faced serious challenges when the financial structures left by Jackson helped bring about the nation's first long-term panic. Van Buren's actions were continuously compared to Jackson's. This was just one problem with being a former incumbent vice president. As one dilemma was solved, another emerged to bother Van Buren throughout his four years in office.

## SUCCEEDING THE GIPPER

Following his formal announcement in October 1987, George Bush launched his second campaign for the presidency. Much had changed in eight years. In 1980, his campaign was an effort to project himself as an alternate to Ronald Reagan. Bush had to convince voters in 1988 that he would continue Reagan's revolution and offer a vision for America's future. Unlike Van Buren, Bush faced opposition in gaining his party's presidential nomination and did not receive the endorsement of Ronald Reagan until after the nomination fight was over.

During the first phase of the campaign, from October 1987 through February 1988, Bush was the object of criticism from Republican hopefuls. Alexander Haig, Ronald Reagan's former secretary of state, was critical of Bush's actions in the Reagan administration. Jack Kemp, the popular congressman from New York, was the ideological heir to Ronald Reagan, but he was not experienced in running a national campaign. Pat Robertson was the president of the Christian Broadcasting Network and the host of the 700 Club. He was one of the leaders of the Christian right, which had gained considerable power within the Republican party, especially among primary voters. Pete Du Pont, the former governor of Delaware, offered a message of concern about the economic problems facing America. Bush's primary opponent was a longtime acquaintance, Senator Robert Dole of Kansas. They had both been loyal supporters of Richard Nixon, but Nixon had replaced Dole as chairman of the Republican National Committee with George Bush in 1972. In 1988, Dole was very popular in the Midwest and spelled trouble for Bush in Iowa.

The second phase of the campaign occurred from February through May when Bush recovered from early disaster and ran away with the Republican nomination. He finally gained Ronald Reagan's endorsement in May. Bush sat back after capturing the nomination to see which Democrat would emerge as challenger. The Democratic race was a three-sided race between Reverend Jesse Jackson, Senator Albert Gore of Tennessee, and Governor Michael Dukakis of Massachusetts, all looking for the momentum to capture the nomination. The New York primary turned to Dukakis, and his path to the nomination was clear. The little-known governor's status grew throughout the primary season, and he led Bush in polls taken in the spring and summer.

The final phase of the campaign was from July through election day November 8, 1988. Bush survived attacks from the Democrats at their convention and pulled even in the polls when the Republicans met to nominate him in August. Bush delivered an excellent acceptance speech, but it was overshadowed by his selection of Senator Dan Quayle as his running mate. Quayle did not have the same liabilities as Richard Johnson, but his problems were considerable. Even with these difficulties, the Bush campaign continued its march, and following Bush's second debate with Dukakis in October, the election seemed to be his. The pollsters were right; George Herbert Walker Bush won a convincing victory and was the man to succeed the Gipper.

As his campaign began in October, Bush's position as vice president was his greatest strength and his greatest weakness. Being closely associated with Ronald Reagan was a major asset that the other contenders had to deal with. Each of the Republicans running for president in 1988 had his own sense of what the Reagan legacy was. The electorate might have questions about the Reagan years, but no Republican could afford to criticize Ronald Reagan personally if he wanted the nomination. Despite the advantage of a close Reagan association, in national polls, the Bush campaign was not doing well in Iowa. Mary McGrory explained in a column in the *Columbus Dispatch*: "It's his association with Ronald Reagan that causes the malaise. Reagan is not popular in a state which has seen nothing of the economic miracle the president boasts of."[59]

On October 29, in Houston, Bush debated the other candidates for the Republican nomination. Bush was the object of attack. Questions surrounding the Intermediate Nuclear Forces (INF) Treaty were posed to Bush.

This treaty, ratified by the Senate in 1988, was an agreement between the United States and the Soviet Union to eliminate their intermediate-range and shorter-range nuclear missiles. This was the first time an entire class of missiles on both sides were eliminated. Pete Du Pont wanted some details from Bush: "We've not seen any vision, any principle, and policy. We're waiting for details, and we're hearing generalities."[60] Haig questioned Bush's support of the INF Treaty when it was first discussed in the cabinet. "I never heard a wimp out of you George."[61] Bush survived these attacks and fired back. According to David Broder in the *Chicago Tribune*, Bush won his first encounter with the other Republican contenders. "This night belonged to Bush—the man who dared to call a Pierre a Pierre," he said.[62] Broder was referring to Bush using Du Pont's first name when he refuted his ideas about reforming Social Security. Du Pont preferred to be called Pete and the use of Pierre helped to project a foreign elitist image to the former Delaware governor. Broder continued his reactions to this first encounter with his fellow Republicans. "He was tough when he needed to be and skillful in evading punches, so he was the clear winner in press room evaluations and in the first round of interviews with voters who watched the debate."[63]

The wimp factor, a term coined by *Time* and other publications, hurt Bush early in the campaign until his confrontation with Dan Rather. Some viewed Bush as a wimp because of his role as vice president and the way he saw that role. As he said, "You can't be an effective or good Vice President unless you're a team player. Some people are cynical about the Vice President's role; they call it buttering up. But I don't believe that. I believe that it's highly responsible to work in a complimentary way with your chief executive."[64] The wimp factor had haunted Bush even prior to him becoming vice president. Ronald Reagan had questioned Bush during the 1980 primary in New Hampshire when he appeared weak in refusing the inclusion of other candidates.

Even with the image problem, George Bush was doing well nationally, except in Iowa. The first primary scheduled for New Hampshire found Bush leading Dole by twenty points in the polls from early November. Bush was also the best organized candidate for the sixteen primaries and caucuses to be held on Super Tuesday, March 8. A solid performance then could decide the nomination very quickly.

Bush was the subject of a five-page story in the *Los Angeles Times* on November 22, 1987, which gained the attention of Washington insider David Broder. *Los Angeles Times* staff writer Barry Bearak, in "Team Player Bush: A Yearning to Serve," used interviews with Bush family members to help reveal Bush's true image as one only desiring to serve his country and to dispel some of the talk of Bush's wimpishness. Bearak offered an interesting comparison between Ronald Reagan and George Bush:

Bush is the genuine article. He was a star baseball player while Ronald Reagan only played one in the movies. He was a daring fighter pilot in the Pacific while Reagan flew simulated missions on the back lots of Culver City. Bush has been married to the same woman for 42 years and has five children who adore him. Reagan is divorced with children he rarely sees. Bush is a devoted churchgoer. Reagan seldom feels the need.[65]

Bearak concluded that Reagan was regarded as a hero by Americans while Bush was judged as being a lap dog or a wimp because of his position as vice president. Bearak offered his opinion on how Bush could win the nomination and the presidency. "To succeed, Bush must take on the future without quarreling with the past, move free of Reagan's shadow without forsaking its shade, lean toward the middle without losing hold of the right."[66]

Bush's role as vice president came under scrutiny in December as new information about Iran/Contra was released. While the investigation continued, a note was released from Admiral John Poindexter, which stated that both Bush and Reagan were firmly behind the arms deal with Iran for the release of hostages. This note contradicted Bush's statement that he did not know that it was an arms for hostages deal. Polls suggested that people still had questions about Bush and Iran/Contra. Alexander Haig took the opportunity to attack Bush's claim that he had been Reagan's copilot for the past seven years. "Bush either wasn't in the cockpit, flew in the wrong direction, or crashed,"[67] he said.

Bush and his staff were also troubled over the publicity and photo opportunity given to Bob Dole when he finally decided to support the INF Treaty. This photo opportunity was with Ronald Reagan in the White House. Bush had supported the treaty from the start, and now Dole was reaping political benefits for his support. President Reagan had promised to remain neutral throughout the primaries, but this event, just weeks before the primary season opened, might have an adverse effect for Bush. As 1987 ended, Bush's candidacy appeared strong if he could survive in Iowa, eliminate the wimp image, and end speculation about Iran/Contra.

Like Van Buren, Bush was the focus of an unauthorized biography. Antony Sutton's *Two Faces of George Bush* hit the market in January, and it studied Bush's entire career. Sutton came to this conclusion: "We have nothing against the gentleman personally, only that we consider Bush to be totally unqualified to be President of the United States."[68] Sutton traced Bush's career and asked many questions about his finances and drug dealers in Central America. Why is Bush considered a wimp? Sutton believed that it was his role as vice president and his strict loyalty to Ronald Reagan. "This cloying loyalty," he wrote, "is taken too far by Bush, so far that it generates an image of indecision."[69]

Sutton also raised questions surrounding Bush and the oil industry; his membership in the Trilateral Commission, a somewhat secret commission organized by David Rockefeller and made up of business and political leaders around the world; and his involvement with drug dealers while acting as Reagan's drug czar. Sutton's book did not have a great effect, although it did enjoy a second printing in June. Sutton went overboard in looking at the Bush family background and associating it with Nazi Germany and Stalin's Russia, as well as making Bush appear to be the drug dealers' best friend. Sutton showed some insight, however, when he explained what difficulties the Bush campaign was experiencing: "The Bush campaign has to face a widespread image of Bush the wimp—Bush seems unable to present himself as a strong leader. The Presidential aura eludes him."[70]

The attacks on Bush's lack of leadership continued as the primary season approached. Bob Dole stated in New Hampshire, "I have a record of leadership, but he doesn't. I assume its getting to him. It's going to be a big issue in this campaign. That's what it's all about: leadership. I can't help it if he hasn't provided any."[71] Of all the candidates to oppose Bush, Bob Dole was the most dangerous. Who was this man that could end Bush's dream once and for all?

### The Dole Threat

Robert Dole had a lot in common with George Bush. Dole did not share Bush's wealthy background, but he was also a hero in World War II. In April 1945, Dole was severely wounded in Northern Italy and nearly died. After years of rehabilitation, Dole still suffers with a useless right arm. His hometown of Russell, Kansas, rallied behind Dole and helped to pay for several operations he needed to appear normal. Dole hoped to return his community's generosity by serving them in Congress. Dole was elected to Congress in 1960 and served in the House of Representatives for eight years. Richard Nixon became a supporter in 1964, and with his help, Dole was elected to the Senate as a loyal Nixonite in 1968.

Dole shared Bush's fondness for Nixon, and he defended the president in the Senate. Dole aspired to be Nixon's running mate in 1972, but he was relegated to operating the Republican National Committee, in part because of his sudden divorce in 1971. Dole was not involved in Watergate, and his divorce did not hamper his reelection campaign in 1974. He was one of the few incumbent Republicans not to face disaster in the midterm elections. Dole became a strong supporter of President Gerald Ford and was given the honor of serving as his running mate in 1976. Dole's attack style worked well, helping to bring Ford back from a thirty-point deficit to almost defeat Jimmy Carter. Dole was criticized, though, for his performance in his debate with Walter Mondale for blaming every war the United States was involved in during the twentieth century on the Democratic party. Ford and Dole were defeated, but Dole was in a strong position to run for president in 1980.

Unlike Bush, who campaigned in 1980 as an alternative to Ronald Reagan, Dole campaigned as one who would continue the conservative cause begun by Reagan in 1976. The public, however, did not turn to the younger Dole. They preferred the real item even if he would be seventy when he became president. Dole finished last in the Iowa caucuses, but he did not want to be the first candidate to withdraw from the race. He remained in the race for the New Hampshire primary and attacked George Bush severely. Reagan recovered to win in New Hampshire and then Dole dropped out and focused on his reelection to the Senate, which he achieved handily.

Dole waited eight years for another opportunity to run for president. He served as an effective Senate minority and majority leader and argued that he knew how to get things done. In Iowa, Dole was from neighboring Kansas, and he was not seen as so closely associated with Reagan as George Bush was. He was a midwesterner and shared midwesterner's beliefs. Dole needed to do well in Iowa; a victory there could be a springboard to the nomination. The Iran/Contra scandal could only help him, and his emphasis on leadership might have its effect on an opponent stuck in the non-leadership office of vice president. Dole's lack of association with Reagan was an asset in Iowa, but a potential liability in the North and South where Reagan was still extremely popular. In a profile in the *National Journal*, columnist Richard Cohen raised this point about Dole: "Whether Dole's emphasis on character, leadership and experience plays well remains to be seen. 'If it doesn't work,' he said before climbing aboard his plane here, 'We'll try something else.' "[72]

Since Bush had to face the occasionally mean-spirited Dole until the Republican nomination, he tried to take the initiative and eliminate Iran/Contra as an issue by answering questions asked by Mary McGrory in an exclusive interview for the *Washington Post* in mid-January 1988. The only issue Bush would not discuss was what he conferred with President Reagan about in private. "I do not discuss what I tell the President."[73] Bush's position on his involvement remained the same. He claimed that he did not know that the arms shipped to Iran were in return for releasing hostages. He stated that if he had known, he would have opposed the deal immediately. Many questions remained, and reporters started to question how difficult a job it was for Bush to be vice president and seek the presidency.

In separate columns in the *Washington Post*, columnist Edwin Yoder and Norman Sherwin discussed the problems of being vice president. Sherwin had been Hubert Humphrey's press secretary when he was vice president and also assisted Humphrey with his memoirs. Sherwin could not think of any great accomplishment made by Humphrey as vice president. "I've had 10 years to think of what Humphrey, whom I idolized, did as V.P. It all adds up to zero."[74] Yoder argued that a vice president simply does nothing including George Bush. "As to high policy, Bush appears to have been a fifth wheel and no more."[75] Sherwin added his depressing description of the vice presidency. "The job of vice president means you are not homeless and you do draw a regular paycheck. Beyond that you are what the president allows you to be, but you have no real authority, no real responsibility and no independent clout. And almost everyone inside knows that."[76]

Also in January, Bush agreed to a live interview with Dan Rather on the *CBS Evening News* for the January 25 broadcast. Bush believed that the broadcast was to be a profile on him; however, it turned out to be an interview focusing on Iran/Contra. After a short video of Bush and his Iran/Contra involvement, the camera then turned to an interview between Rather and Bush. The interview was heated, with Rather interrupting Bush on several occasions. The interview became nasty when Bush made this response to Rather: "I don't think it's fair to judge a whole career, it's not fair to judge my whole career by a rehash on Iran. How would you like it if I judged your whole career by those seven minutes when you walked off the set in New York, would you like that?"[77] Rather angrily continued his questions on Iran/Contra and concluded that many questions were left unanswered. He suggested to Bush that he should have a press conference prior to the Iowa caucuses. Bush responded: "I've been to 86 news conferences since March, 86 of 'em since March."[78] Rather then ended the interview: "I gather that the answer is no. Thank you very much for being with us Mr. Vice President."[79]

Bush's nine minutes with Rather did more to eliminate the wimp image and discussion on Iran/Contra than anything he did previously. Polls taken showed respondents' beliefs that Rather had mistreated the vice president. Bush stated immediately following the interview: "The bastard didn't lay a glove on me."[80] A poll taken by *Time* found that 42 percent believed that Bush came out ahead in the exchange as opposed to 27 percent for Rather.[81] The confrontation with Rather seemed to bring new life to the Bush campaign; however, it did not help Bush in Iowa, where Reagan was unpopular. Bush's display of emotion and his willingness to take the offensive helped to dispel the wimp image once and for all. Bush had quieted two concerns raised about him. He now had to face the decision of the voters in Iowa. Another victory like the one in 1980 was out of the question, but a strong second would keep his boat sailing straight toward the nomination.

In Iowa, Dole won easily with 38 percent of the vote. Surprisingly, Bush finished third behind Pat Robertson with just 19 percent of the vote. Bush led in polls nationwide, but lost terribly in Iowa. Dole's campaign manager, Bill Brock, declared following the Iowa victory: "This is a devastating result for the vice president."[82] Polls in New Hampshire suddenly saw the race too close to call after Bush had enjoyed a twenty-point lead throughout

the fall and winter. Bush needed a victory in New Hampshire or his candidacy was in trouble.

While Dole continued to attack Bush on his lack of leadership, Bush
pulled out all the stops in New Hampshire. He would not sit back in Texas
for almost a week as he did in 1980 and take victory for granted. Bush
planned to "do a better job of getting my message out. Work harder,
though I don't know how I can do that."[83] Once again, Bush was the
subject of articles on the difficulty a vice president had when seeking the
presidency. Veteran Washington reporter Haynes Johnson compared Bush
to other vice presidents in the *Washington Post* following Iowa: "None of
this means that Bush's political fate is ordained. It does mean that he is in
danger of falling into the familiar and fatal pattern of those who have tried
following Van Buren's path to the top."[84]

Bush's campaign manager in New Hampshire was Governor John Sun-
unu. He carefully orchestrated every step for Bush in the Granite State.
Unlike in Iowa, Ronald Reagan was immensely popular in New Hampshire, and Bush could count on a boost from his association with the hero
of many New Hampshire voters. Bush aired ads attacking Dole for refusing
to oppose tax increases, which angered Dole, who was tired of Bush lying
about his record. An angry Dole was seen on television, which hurt him a
lot. The night before the primary, the Bush team flew in Barry Goldwater,
the father of the conservative movement, to endorse George Bush in an
election eve commercial: "I believe in George Bush. He's the man to continue the conservative revolution we started 24 years ago."[85]

Dole had difficulty continuing the momentum he gained from Iowa. Bush
was better organized, and Dole had to change his message to suit an area
that still loved Ronald Reagan. On election day, Bush made a tremendous
comeback, defeating Dole by nine points, 38 percent to 29 percent. Following his primary victory, Bush announced: "I have a lot in common with
Mark Twain; reports of my death are greatly exaggerated."[86] The Dole
camp learned a lesson about George Bush in New Hampshire. David Keene,
a Dole consultant said: "If we learned anything it's that we're going to
have to knock him down. He won't fall down by himself."[87] The campaign
now moved to the South for Super Tuesday on March 8, 1988. Bush had
all the advantages in the states holding primaries and caucuses on that day.
Dole would have to pull off some surprises or his candidacy would be in
peril.

The press took another look at Bush and Dole and decided that both
men represented the Republican establishment. Political reporter Nicholas
Leman looked back at the Nixon years when Bush and Dole became aware
of each other. Nixon replaced Dole as RNC chairman with Bush because
he was viewed as being more moderate and loyal to the president. A meeting between John Ehrlichman and the president revealed the following

opinion from Nixon: "Eliminate the politicians, except George Bush. He'd do anything for the cause."[88] Both men began their rise at the same time, but Bush continued to be viewed as the loyal one.

The press began to analyze Bush's message carefully. David Hoffman, covering Bush for the *Washington Post*, gave this observation of Bush's commitment to arms control agreements with the Soviet Union, reducing the deficit, and his desire to become the education president: "Bush seems to be offering essentially a third Reagan term."[89] On Super Tuesday, Hoffman concluded that "Bush has been running a campaign based entirely on symbols and devoid of substance."[90] Whether or not that charge was true, Bush swept Super Tuesday, winning sixteen of the seventeen primaries and caucuses. Bush's only setback came in Washington where he was defeated by Pat Robertson. Dole's candidacy was in danger, but he continued to the Illinois primary. The South had remained loyal to Ronald Reagan and George Bush. "I can beat George Bush, but I cannot beat Ronald Reagan,"[91] Dole said.

Following Super Tuesday, Jack Kemp, who was considered the darling of the right, offered this opinion: "There is no doubt in my mind that Bush and Dole represent the old guard of the Republican Party, the establishment of the Republican Party. And the Revolution as we know it is over."[92] Dole campaigned in Illinois on the theme that he could garner more support from Reagan Democrats and Independents than Bush. Polls showing that Bush was trailing the Democrats if the election was held then seemed to support Dole's argument.

No upset, however, occurred in Illinois. Bush trounced Dole 54 to 36 percent. His nomination was a virtual certainty, and there were calls for Dole to withdraw from the race. Dole admitted on March 26, 1988, that Bush would be the likely nominee: "We need to keep a Republican in the White House. That's where I'm coming from. And if it can't be me, it will be George Bush."[93] Dole withdrew from the race three days later. Bush could now turn his attention to important matters, such as selecting a running mate and formulating a strategy to defeat the Democratic nominee.

Political columnist Mark Shields discussed Bush's options for selecting a running mate in the *Washington Post*. Shields noted what philosopher Alan Baron called the Discomfort Rule: If a candidate selects a running mate who does not anger his supporters, then he has made the wrong choice. In Bush's case, Shields concluded that "Bush does not need to reassure any group or interest. What Bush must instead demonstrate are his own leadership and self confidence to show voters he is truly his own man, that he is unconcerned about being upstaged by a strong and independent running mate."[94] Regarding strategy for the upcoming fall season, Bush made this statement in early April: "I'm convinced that whoever the nominee is, we're going to have a very clear difference on the issues, so I will continue to talk about broad themes."[95]

## The Democratic Opposition

At this point in April, the Democratic nomination was still in doubt, with Jesse Jackson, Albert Gore, and Michael Dukakis fighting it out. How did these three emerge in a party that had Gary Hart as its front-runner throughout 1987 and Mario Cuomo waiting in the wings, like Henry Clay in 1836, ready to enter the race and capture the presidency?

Gary Hart had done well in primaries against Walter Mondale in 1984 and had resigned his Senate seat in 1986 to run for the presidency. Disaster struck Hart when photographers caught him with another woman after he had told them to follow him. Reporters had questioned Hart about the strength of his marriage and that was when he suggested that they follow him if they had any doubts. Hart withdrew from the race and then later returned, but he was never the same candidate. Hart's departure put the spotlight on obscure candidates who became known as the seven dwarfs. Senator Joseph Biden had an opportunity to capture the public's attention, but thanks to Dukakis staffer John Sasso, Biden's campaign collapsed because of allegations of plagiarism. Sasso publicized videotapes of Biden and British politician Neil Kinnoch speaking. It was evident that Biden used some of Kinnoch's phrases in his own speeches.

As 1988 dawned, Jesse Jackson was the best known of the Democratic hopefuls. Calls were made to summon Mario Cuomo to the stage, but Cuomo did not answer the call. He remained out of the race because he argued that he could not run for president and be an effective governor, but until Dukakis captured enough delegates, the possibility of a Cuomo draft remained. A race quickly developed between Dukakis and Jackson after Missouri Congressman Richard Gephardt's poor showing in New Hampshire. Gephardt had won the Iowa caucuses but, like Dole, was unable to capitalize on early success. When the campaign turned south, Senator Albert Gore of Tennessee became a player. Following Super Tuesday, the three men were about even in delegates. It appeared that Dukakis would either win the nomination or a brokered convention would occur. In many minds, Jesse Jackson was just unelectable. The key contest took place in New York, where Michael Dukakis defeated his two rivals and finally saw his way to the nomination.

Dukakis was a three-term governor of Massachusetts and took credit for what he claimed was an economic miracle in his state. In his profile in the *National Journal*, Ronald Brownstein remarked, "Dukakis is seen in some circles as the great liberal hope on this plate of nouvelles Democrats."[96] Dukakis offered change from the Reagan years because he believed that many Americans had been left behind. Dukakis may have been a successful governor, but he had some liabilities. "His rhetoric, like his governing style, has an unflamboyant compact quality to it. He doesn't 'excite passion,' "

Democratic pollster Brad Bowan noted, adding that he did generate confidence in his competence.[97]

Dukakis' hope for victory was to maintain the traditional New Deal coalition and attract some Reagan Democrats back because of his competence. Brownstein concluded, "His appeal is aimed at the head, not the heart—but in easily accessible language that comes across more like unforced conversation than calculated political speech, especially on TV."[98] After eight years of the "Great Communicator," Dukakis was counting on the public to support a candidate who promised to get the job done as he saw it. Dukakis also had the added pressure of being an incumbent governor. He did not like his lieutenant governor, so after the Democratic convention, Dukakis spent a great deal of time in Massachusetts and not on the campaign trail spreading his message of competence.

### The Reagan Endorsement

While Dukakis was firming his grasp on the Democratic nomination, Bush was mending fences and preparing for the upcoming campaign. Bush met with Dole, ending their personal battle and beginning speculation that Dole might be Bush's running mate. Bush also received advice for the general election from the staff of Senator Dan Evans of Washington. They advised that Bush should "draw a stronger picture of who you are to the people of the country. We are looking for a president of competence, experience and ability."[99] Evans' staff continued in its letter with more advice for Bush: "Don't squander your credibility on issues like school prayer and a balanced budget amendment, but rather focus on those programs which can bring new hope to people and new opportunity for our free enterprise system."[100] Evans' staff gave their suggestions to Bush on Iran/Contra, which he rejected outright: "Go to the president and ask his approval to tell the whole story including the advice you may have given him in your private meetings."[101]

Bush's staff began preparations for the Republican convention in August and the upcoming endorsement by Ronald Reagan at the beginning of May. Throughout the primary season, Bush operated without Reagan's endorsement, but he still took credit for the accomplishments of the Reagan administration. Bush's staff now wanted to orchestrate carefully Reagan's official statement of endorsement and his appearance at the Republican National Convention in order to make Bush appear independent but still pursuing the same goals as Reagan. Plans were made for Reagan to arrive in New Orleans for the first night of the convention and then leave the rest of the week for Bush to offer his plan for America and how he would continue the course charted by his predecessor. Some difficulty, however, arose over the formal endorsement of Ronald Reagan.

Reagan was scheduled to endorse Bush at a GOP congressional fundraiser on May 11, 1988. Reagan gave his endorsement at the end of his speech:

If I may. I'd like to take a moment to say just a word about my future plans. In doing so, I'll break a silence I've maintained for some time with regard to the presidential candidates. I intend to campaign as hard as I can. My candidate is a former member of Congress, ambassador to China, ambassador to the United Nations, director of the CIA, and national chairman of the Republican Party. I'm going to work as hard as I can to make Vice President Bush the next president of the United States.[102]

Many Republicans and political pundits viewed this endorsement as lukewarm. Apparently Bush knew about and approved of Reagan's remarks prior to the speech, but the perception remained that Reagan was less than enthusiastic. Reagan responded to this perception the following day by issuing another statement regarding Bush. "He has my full confidence and total support. I will campaign actively on his behalf."[103] Bush had finally received Reagan's endorsement, but some questioned how helpful it would be.

### On to the Convention

Bush's public campaigning came to halt as his staff made plans for the fall of 1988. Polls found Bush trailing Michael Dukakis, but the election was still six months away. The polling aside, the *Washington Post* published the findings of Allan Lichtman in late April. Lichtman was a political historian at American University who developed a model to predict presidential elections. His model had successfully predicted every election since 1860. Lichtman's model predicted that 1988 would belong to George Bush. In Chapter 4 of this book, models used by Lichtman and other political scientists will be analyzed to explain the victories of Van Buren and Bush.

The vice president spent the summer months trying to avoid the mess surrounding Attorney General Ed Messe and the failed efforts to remove Manuel Noriega from power in Panama. For over a year, the attorney general had been the subject of an ethics investigation. The Democrats viewed this investigation as yet more evidence of the unethical behavior in the Reagan administration. Meese announced in July that he would resign and was not indicted.

In January, Noriega refused an American request to resign as the leader of Panama's military and allow free elections to take place. In the spring, Noriega was charged with drug crimes for assisting the importation of drugs into the United States. George Bush was involved because he had met with Noriega while he was America's drug czar. Bush denied any personal knowledge of Noriega's activities and did not suffer any repercussions from either incident. Although polls showed him trailing, and by seventeen points in California, Bush remained calm. "I don't worry about it; the election is five and a half months away. The thing hasn't really started in terms of Democrats versus Republicans and we haven't gotten any of that in focus, and it won't be until after the convention."[104]

Bush began to voice some attacks against Michael Dukakis in mid-June. Columnist George Will argued early in the month why the Republicans should be happy and the Democrats concerned. "Republicans have done what parties dream of doing. They have decorously nominated the consensus choice of most party leaders in a context of peace and prosperity. Democrats have done precisely what recent history warns against: they have nominated a northeastern liberal."[105] Will predicted what Bush's strategy would be. "Clearly, the Bush campaign's premise is that Bush should not count on persuading the public to vote for him. Rather, he should frighten the public into voting against Michael Dukakis. Bush wants to Goldwaterize Dukakis."[106]

In his attacks on Dukakis, Bush used the issue of crime, especially the furlough system in Massachusetts. Initially, Senator Albert Gore had questioned this system during the primaries. Bush began attacking Dukakis on June 19, 1988, for allowing violent criminals to go on unsupervised weekend furloughs. Three days later, Bush provided the details of the Horton case. Willie Horton was a convicted murderer who escaped while on furlough and then raped a woman and stabbed her companion in Maryland. Horton had been granted a furlough, although he was not eligible for parole. Bush gave his impression of Massachusetts' furlough system: "So I'm opposed to these unsupervised weekend furloughs for first degree murderers who have not, who are not eligible for parole. Put me down against that."[107] Everyone was exposed to television ads with the face of Willie Horton and a revolving door representing the Massachusetts prison system under Michael Dukakis.

Dukakis never fully or convincingly defended the furlough program. He first argued that many states had similar programs. He later argued that he signed legislation to repeal such furloughs. The truth was that legislation repealing furloughs was passed after pressure from the Horton case forced the issue. The Willie Horton story haunted Dukakis on television and on the radio throughout the campaign. His perceived weakness on crime was again and again presented to the public.

Dukakis also faced attack for the condition of Boston Harbor. The harbor was so polluted that the Reagan administration had sued Massachusetts to clean it up in the mid-1980s. Dukakis, who campaigned on the Massachusetts miracle, spent considerable time explaining instances where the miracle apparently had failed to materialize.

Dukakis' staff did not sit back; it searched for weapons to use against George Bush. This was the same staff that had destroyed the campaign of

Joseph Biden in the winter. In late June, columnists Jack Anderson and Dale Van Atta discussed the investigative work of the Dukakis staff into George Bush's tenure as the nation's drug czar. Dukakis' staff concluded that "the vice president's eight years as drug czar of the Reagan administration were window dressing."[108] The staff did not make the allegations that Antony Sutton made in his biography of Bush—that he was involved in the importation of drugs—but there was evidence that could have damaged the vice president. Dukakis for no apparent reason never used this information in a way to score political points.

George Bush was very busy in July. Preparations continued for the convention in August and Bush stepped up the process of selecting a running mate. Bush continued his attacks on Dukakis, but the vice president did not want to be seen as always on the attack; "People want to feel better about things like homelessness, education, child care, and narcotics. They want to see progress and progress means change. But they don't want radical change, or fundamental liberal change."[109]

The press started to question even before the nominating convention whether a Bush victory necessarily meant a mandate to continue the Reagan years. Thomas Edsall reported: "Bush faces the danger of winning the election without the kind of crosscutting mandate that gave Reagan in the early years of his first term the power to set and enact a comprehensive national agenda."[110] A way to hold on to the Reagan legacy was to select a popular vice president who might provide Bush with the needed mandate.

Suggestions for running mates came from many directions. Columnists Evans and Novak raised several names, but they believed that ultimately Bush and his staff would decide between Bob Dole and Jack Kemp. "They want a running mate for Bush who has been bloodied in the presidential campaign arena, and since no insider considers Howard Baker desirable, that means Dole or Kemp."[111] George Will offered three suggestions for possible running mates for Bush. Will named Alan Simpson, the popular senator from Wyoming, and a close friend of the vice president; Colin Powell, the national security advisor and who, if selected, would be the first black on a national ticket; and Peter Uueberroth, the former baseball commissioner and organizer of the 1984 Summer Olympics. Each man had potential, but only if Bush was worried about his election. Debate in the press continued until Bush's surprise selection during the Republican National Convention.

In July 1988, the Democrats held their convention in Atlanta and nominated Michael Dukakis for president. His selection for a running mate was Texas senator Lloyd Bentsen, the same man who defeated George Bush in the 1970 Texas senate race. Bush was the subject of attacks during the convention, especially from Edward Kennedy and Ann Richards of Texas. Kennedy went through Bush's career and ended each stage with the refrain "Where was George?" During her remarks, Richards claimed that Bush could not help himself from making misstatements, since "he was born with a silver foot in his mouth." Dukakis emerged from the convention slightly ahead in the polls. Following the convention, Dukakis went home to Massachusetts to run the state, allowing Bush to set the agenda of the campaign.

As Bush was planning for August, it looked as though Reagan might actively campaign for Bush. Lou Cannon, in *Newsday*, argued that Reagan would not take a back seat as President Eisenhower did during the 1960 campaign. "Reagan's friends say he genuinely cares for Bush and wants to do all that he can to push him over the top in November."[112] Reagan's popularity was a great asset for Bush. The July unemployment figures were the lowest since 1974, and Reagan had ended problems surrounding his attorney general by accepting Ed Meese's resignation and appointing Richard Thornburgh to take his place.

Bush seemed to be drawing closer to Reagan as the convention approached. Bush's campaign manager, Lee Atwater, stated: "Ronald Reagan is still one of the most popular political figures in the country and his involvement in the campaign is a big plus for the vice president."[113] Bush's aides also noticed Dukakis' reluctance to attack the president directly. Reagan's campaigning could keep many Reagan Democrats in the fold. Dukakis campaign manager Susan Estrich responded, "Our overall position is we are neither running with nor against Reagan, we are running for the future."[114] President Reagan could enjoy taking shots at Dukakis without having to fear retaliation.

The next task at hand was for Bush to select a running mate. The Bush campaign began background checks on possible candidates late in July, and Richard Nixon suggested that Bush should release a long list of possibilities to keep the press guessing. Bush released a list with seventeen names, including for the first time Senator Dan Quayle of Indiana. One columnist suggested that Bush should ask Ronald Reagan to be his running mate, but nothing came from this suggestion. The *Washington Post* released information that the Bush campaign had done polling with possible running mates and discovered that no one boosted the ticket nationally, but only in the home state of each candidate.

Just days before the convention, Evans and Novak took a look at Bush's short list and they argued the pros and cons of each man or woman. When it came to Senator Dan Quayle, they wrote, "Sen. Dan Quayle of Indiana, a national security specialist, is totally acceptable to conservatives, but generates limited enthusiasm."[115] Bush's selection was unknown, but there were rumblings that conservative delegates would nominate their own candidate if they objected to Bush's selection. The delegates had to wait a couple of days as the Republican National Convention opened its doors in New Orleans.

*Time* devoted its August 22, 1988, issue to George Bush and the upcoming campaign. The feature article written by Laurence Barret stated that

Bush could not win without relying on the popularity of Ronald Reagan: "Yet as the crown prince, the authorized inheritor of the Reaganite mantle, Bush may still be able to rally the faithful behind the implicit message of 'Four More Years!' "[116] The article continued to describe how important Ronald Reagan would be in November. Either Bush or Dukakis would have to contend with his legacy, which includes the rising national debt. Bush seemed to be the man to continue the legacy. "That would be the final irony of Reagan's legacy: a Bush presidency destroyed by the very ideology that allowed him to fill in the final line of his résumé."[117]

Bush seemed to understand what he had to do to win in November. "I will win because people won't want to gamble and go back to the Jimmy Carter days and the failed policies of the past."[118] Finally, Bush's old patron Richard Nixon offered his own opinion of the upcoming campaign. "The 1988 election is not about style any more than it is about competence or breeding. It is about two starkly different visions of America and how it should be led into the 21st century."[119] George Bush was ready to go to New Orleans and show that he was the best man to continue the Reagan legacy into the future.

The opening night of the convention was devoted to Ronald Reagan. It was an opportunity for Republicans to thank Reagan for leading them for the past eight years. Reagan promised to campaign hard for Bush and then suddenly left the scene for his vice president. Bush arrived the following day in New Orleans. The remaining time at the convention was for George Bush to grab the attention of Americans and launch the fall campaign.

The most powerful speech in support of Bush came from former President Gerald Ford. The former president directly rebuked the speech Ted Kennedy gave at the Democratic convention. "I will be damned if I will stand by and let anyone with a smirk and a sneer discredit the honor, service, accountability, and competence of George Bush."[120] Following Ford's powerful speech, Bush was nominated for president. As this was all taking place, questions were arising about Bush's selection of Dan Quayle as his running mate. Earlier in the day, Bush introduced Quayle to the public. The event was planned poorly and Quayle appeared too energetic.

While Quayle did not have the liabilities of Van Buren's Richard Johnson, his problems were considerable. The main problem was his enlistment in the Indiana National Guard in an effort to avoid service in the Vietnam War. When it was learned that Quayle's father exerted pressure to get his son in, some wondered whether Bush should dump Quayle and select someone else. Bush remained loyal to Quayle and would not drop him from the ticket.

Dan Quayle had more experience in government in 1988 than Geraldine Ferraro had in 1984. He was a two-term congressman and, in 1988, was in the middle of his second term in the Senate. Quayle came from a powerful family in Indiana and had enjoyed a pampered upbringing. He rode the coattails of Ronald Reagan in 1980 and defeated longtime senator Birch Bayh. His record in both houses of Congress was not impressive. Quayle was very conservative and a staunch supporter of Ronald Reagan. That helped him win reelection in 1986, when he enjoyed the largest victory in Indiana's history.

How did Quayle gain the nomination from Bush when he was not very well known outside of Indiana? David Broder and Bob Woodward of Watergate fame studied this question in their book *The Man Who Would Be President: Dan Quayle*. They argued that although Quayle was a virtual unknown nationally, he was well known to Bush and his advisers. Two of Bush's aides ran Quayle's reelection campaign, and they strongly sang his praises to Bush. "His selection was the happy result of months of subtle, even stealthy planning—a quality not commonly associated with his name," Broder and Woodward wrote.[121] The reasons given at the time for Quayle's selection were his conservative credentials, his midwestern background, and his generational appeal. At only forty-two, Quayle was seen as a way for Bush to bridge the age gap. Quayle survived his rocky start and left New Orleans for an uncertain future on the campaign trail. With the Quayle issue behind him for now, George Bush delivered the most important speech of his life, accepting the Republican nomination he had coveted for more than eight years.

Bush gave a wonderful performance on the evening of August 18, 1988, promising no new taxes and a kinder and gentler America. He did not forget to include Ronald Reagan in his text: "For seven and a half years, I have helped the president conduct the most difficult job on earth. Ronald Reagan asked for and received my candor. He never asked for, but he did receive my loyalty."[122] Bush also had no difficulty including himself in the accomplishments of the Reagan administration:

Eight years ago, I stood here with Ronald Reagan and we promised together to break with the past and return America to her greatness. Eight years later, look at what the American people have produced—the highest level of economic growth in our entire history and the lowest level of world tensions in more than fifty years.[123]

In his speech, Bush also incorporated rhetoric used by Franklin Roosevelt in 1940: "My friends, these days the world moves even more quickly, and now, after two great terms, a switch will be made. But when you have to changes horses in midstream doesn't it make sense to switch to one who's going the same way."[124]

Bush promised to take his message throughout the country. "I will keep America moving forward, always forward—for a better America, for an endless, ending dream and a thousand points of light. This is my mission, and I will complete it."[125] Bush left New Orleans with just one hurdle left in his way to the presidency. He had to take on Michael Dukakis head to head to reach his final goal.

Bush received rave reviews for his speech written by Peggy Noonan, who was brought in to the Bush camp to improve the vice president's style. The only criticism leveled at Bush was his selection of Quayle as his running mate. Many viewed Dan Quayle as too young, too inexperienced, and a political lightweight concerned more about his golf game than anything else. Polls suggested that the public had difficulties picturing Quayle as president, unlike Dukakis's respected running mate Lloyd Bentsen. Quayle's selection puzzled Broder, who, otherwise, had praise for Bush's probable cabinet members. "Unlike Quayle, they are people with strong academic, political and (in many cases) business credentials—exemplars, in most cases, of the self same Republican establishment that produced Bush."[126] Quayle did not seem not to fit.

## The General Campaign

The general election campaign traditionally gets under way after Labor Day. By the second week in September, Bush was ahead in the polls. What had happened to Dukakis' double digit lead of the spring? Dukakis had remained at home running Massachusetts throughout August because he did not trust his lieutenant governor; consequently, he did not respond to Bush's attacks on the furlough program, the pollution of Boston Harbor, or the pledge of allegiance issue. During the 1988 campaign the issue of flag burning and perhaps a constitutional amendment outlawing this form of protest was discussed. Dukakis opposed such an amendment and did not think that children should be forced to take the pledge of allegiance either. Bush, then, was able to label Dukakis as a liberal without a fight.

George Will attempted to explain what had gone wrong for Dukakis since the Democratic convention. "The bounce Dukakis got from his convention was remarkably short lived. Why? In the last half of the primary season Dukakis was, in the eyes of many Democratic voters, less Dukakis than Mr. Not Jesse Jackson."[127] Dukakis seemed to move away from Jackson and not encourage his active campaigning. Will suggested putting a populist spin on Dukakis' economic message and stop harping on Iran/Contra or Manuel Noriega: "Any votes that will be won on those issues have long since been won."[128]

Dukakis finally returned to the campaign trail after Labor Day and accused Bush of using Joe McCarthy tactics in his television ads. He tried to return the focus of the election on what he believed it should be. "This election is a choice between leadership that's out of touch with real people and leadership that shares your values and stands on your side,"[129] he said. Dukakis also emphasized the differences between the running mates, Bentsen and Quayle. This tactic would work if the voters went to the polls concerned with the bottom spot on the ticket. Dukakis hoped to use this comparison to his advantage during his debates with Bush and in Bentsen's debate with Quayle.

Ronald Reagan kept his promise and began actively campaigning for Bush. For political observers, this was an occurrence that had not happened in recent memory. A president and a nominee had not worked together during the campaigns of 1960 and 1968. When the campaign ended, Ronald Reagan had traveled to sixteen states, logged over 25,000 miles, and delivered thirty-five speeches for Bush. Reagan's approval rating rose to 60 percent by November, and there was hope that some of this support would be transferred to Bush. White House press secretary Marlin Fitzwater described what effects Reagan's campaigning might have: "It's hard to say if the president's popularity translates directly but it does translate into the idea that the economy is sound and the administration is a success. This bolsters the basic tenet of the Bush campaign that we are the change."[130]

The campaign faced a possible turning point when Bush and Dukakis met in their first debate. A poll prior to the debate showed Bush with solid leads in states totaling 235 electoral votes to just 138 for Dukakis. The Massachusetts governor needed a strong performance to start turning the tide. Dukakis performed well but did not land any knockout punches. Bush defended himself well and was able to keep the liberal label on his opponent. The vice president's closing remarks asked for the public's support while Dukakis just talked about a great future for America. The former wimp now appeared to be the stronger candidate. Bush remarked, "In the final analysis, a person goes into a voting booth, they're going to say, who has the values I believe in? Who has the integrity and the stability to get the job done? My fellow Americans, I am that man, and I ask for your support."[131] Polls taken suggested that the debate was about even. Dukakis did creep closer in national surveys as the attention now turned to the vice-presidential debate.

Bush's running mate had not been in the spotlight since the convention. David Hoffman for the *Washington Post* discussed what Quayle had been doing for the past two months. "Quayle has been given a relatively light schedule, such as two rallies a day and two private fund-raisers and infrequent news conferences."[132] Quayle's debate with Lloyd Bentsen was a great opportunity for him to establish his credibility as a candidate.

Quayle often compared himself to John Kennedy, since they were about the same age when they sought national office. In some areas, Quayle actually had more experience in government than Kennedy. His handlers instructed Quayle not to raise this comparison during the debate. Quayle disregarded the advice and raised the comparison anyway. Lloyd Bentsen responded with one of the most memorable lines from the campaign. "I knew Jack Kennedy. Senator, you are no Jack Kennedy." Bentsen clearly won the debate, but it did not translate into a surge in the polls. Quayle was once again relegated to the backseat to run a quiet campaign in Republican strongholds.

Michael Dukakis had one more opportunity against George Bush on October 13, 1988. Polls released prior to the second debate found Bush clearly ahead in twenty-eight states with Dukakis leading in just seven. Richard Stengel covered the Dukakis campaign for *Time*. He was allowed to view Dukakis' preparation for the second debate, and, after the election, he reported what happened. The Dukakis camp was concerned, and staffers convinced him to attack Bush on six subjects. "Quayle, Iran/Contra, abortion, patriotism, drugs and Boston Harbor. He was also supposed to dare the Vice President to look directly into the camera and tell the American people that J. Danforth Quayle was best qualified to be Vice President."[133] Dukakis raised only one of these subjects, and his defeat seemed certain. What happened to these carefully laid plans?

Dukakis woke the morning of the debate not feeling well and with a sore throat. He took a couple of naps during the day and canceled his practice session. When he arrived for the debate, Dukakis was not in his best form. The first question asked to him by Bernard Shaw made him appear unfeeling and set the tone for the rest of the night. Shaw asked Dukakis if he would support the death penalty if his wife Kitty was raped and murdered. Dukakis responded that he would not support the death penalty even in this instance. Dukakis did not recover. He was seen as the clear loser of the second debate.

Following the debate, *Newsweek* studied why Bush was leading in the polls. "Much of his strength traces to the national optimism about the economy and to Ronald Reagan's resurgent popularity, and there is little that Dukakis can do about that."[134] Dukakis still had a few weeks, and his staff worked on a eighteen-state strategy to capture the presidency. Dukakis campaigned tirelessly in the North and Midwest, and he finally proclaimed that he was proud to be labeled as a liberal.

Reagan went twice to California to help bring the state in for Bush. The president was well received everywhere he campaigned, and he usually left each campaign stop with this message. "If you would, I hope you'll win just one more for the Gipper."[135] Bush also tirelessly campaigned in the Midwest and in Texas. He made this statement while campaigning with Gerald Ford in Michigan: "If I win this election, it will be a rejection of the failed liberal policies in the past and a confirmation of your beliefs in these traditional American values."[136] Reagan ended his campaign swing with a stop in Texas. "Although come January, I'm going to be riding off into the sunset, I feel a little like, I'm a little on the ballot myself this year."[137]

On election eve, it appeared that George Bush would win the next day.

Many in the press were not happy with this expected result. The *Washington Post* refused to endorse a candidate, and the editors of *The New Republic* endorsed Michael Dukakis despite his miserable campaign:

Dukakis has run a miserable campaign, incompetently failing to rebut Bush's calumines, yet driven by desperation into misrepresentations and phony issues of his own. His insistence after nomination that the campaign would be about "competency" not "ideology" was a failure of nerve that sadly has turned into its own fitting punishment.[138]

Bush offered his final message on election eve with a familiar refrain. "Americans are better off than they were eight years ago and if you elect me president, you will be better off four years from now than you are today."[139] It was now left to the voters to decide whether they agreed with the message that had been spread by Bush for over a year.

George Bush won the election with forty states and 426 electoral votes to ten states and 112 electoral votes for Michael Dukakis. Bush won the popular vote with 54 percent to 46 percent for Dukakis. After more than 150 years, George Bush triumphed over the dilemma that had blocked every vice president since Martin Van Buren. Following Dukakis' concession speech, Bush met with his supporters to proclaim victory and to thank Ronald Reagan. "I thank him for turning our country around and for being my friend and for going the extra mile on the hustings. He is simply one of the most decent men I have ever met."[140] Bush then went on to tell the American people that he wanted to bring everyone together and to work with Congress. At a press conference the day after the election, President-elect Bush gave thanks to Martin Van Buren: "I also want to thank Martin Van Buren for paving the way. It's been a long time Marty."[141]

Michael Dukakis had done the best for a Democrat since 1980. He won nine more states than Walter Mondale in 1984, but many Democrats blamed his poor organization for the party's defeat. Dukakis expressed an alternative view. "I think the American people are saying that they want continuity in the presidency."[142] Exit polls seemed to confirm Dukakis' opinion. Polls suggested that a large majority of voters who valued experience voted for Bush. Another large majority of voters who approved of President Reagan's office performance placed their ballots for Bush as well.

Bush met with President Reagan the following day to thank him and to begin the transition process. Like Van Buren in 1836, he kept many of Reagan's cabinet members in the new Bush administration. Reagan stated in his meeting with Bush, "This is not the end of an era, but a time to refresh and strengthen our new beginning. In fact, to those who sometimes flatter me with talk of a Reagan revolution today my hope is this: You ain't seen nothing yet."[143]

Some political pundits attributed Bush's victory to the effective use of negative advertising. One cannot question the effect of Willie Horton and the picture of the polluted Boston Harbor. Others point to Bush's proximity to Ronald Reagan for his victory. But being associated with a popular president is not enough, as Richard Nixon found out in 1960. Bush had successfully become his own man since the Republican convention. He was no longer everyone's second choice. The campaign of George Bush in 1988 was not one of a wimp. The effective use of the media had made George Bush the choice to defend America from enemies foreign and domestic and to continue the Reagan legacy.

The press and the opposition questioned whether Bush had a mandate during the transition period. The almost unanimous position was that he did not. Senator Bill Bradley of New Jersey claimed: "Bush has no mandate. He ran on very little and Congress will control the legislative and political agenda."[144] Columnists raised comparisons between Van Buren and Bush and wondered whether Bush would face the same disaster that befell Van Buren when he became president. Economic problems struck the nation in 1837 and Van Buren took the blame and would not be reelected in 1840.

Inauguration day January 20, 1989, was a far nicer day than the frigid day that greeted Ronald Reagan's second inaugural. Martin Van Buren was the first president not to have fought for America's freedom. George Bush might be the last president to have fought in World War II. As Bush started his address, "A New Breeze Is Blowing," the new president of the United States began by thanking his predecessor. "There is a man here who has earned a lasting place in our hearts—and in our history. President Reagan on behalf of our nation, I thank you for the wonderful things that you have done for America."[145]

After his address, Bush and his wife Barbara, along with the Quayles, said goodbye to Ronald and Nancy Reagan. As the former president flew off in a helicopter, there was sadness for those who grew up while Reagan was president or had followed his political career for almost thirty years. Reagan's day in the limelight had finally come to an end. A new day dawned with the loyal George Bush at the helm. The dilemma that had haunted Richard Nixon and Hubert Humphrey had finally been resolved.

# 4

# Explaining the Victories

Martin Van Buren and George Bush had overcome the vice presidential dilemma and were elected president of the United States. They both bene-fited from serving as vice presidents to popular two-term presidents. Is there any way to explain why they were elected other than through similarities between two men separated by over a century and a half? Political scientists offer three models to explain voting behavior that show a greater correlation between Van Buren and Bush than just historical coincidence. The three models are cyclical, prospective, and retrospective.

Richard Ellis and Aaron Wildavsky offer a study of presidential leadership, which shows the balancing act a president must maintain between cultural impulses in the United States to hold on to political power. Stephen Skowronek shows how presidents function and the methods that result in a new president taking the helm and functioning in a different manner. Erwin Hargrove and Michael Nelson similarly argue in their study how a preceding president sets the stage for the next. They argue that whether a leader concerns himself with preparation, achievement, or consolidation, the incumbent president apparently dictates the success of his successor. James David Barber provides a study that shows that voting behavior falls into twelve-year cycles. The elections of Van Buren and Bush happened to fall during the same cycle.

A different approach is taken by the final two works using a retrospective model, which directly explains why people vote the way they do. Allan Lichtman and Ken DeCell's work establishes thirteen keys to being elected president. Their simple formula has correctly predicted the result of every presidential election since 1860. The basis for the keys is the performance of the incumbent administration. This method of looking at past performance originated with the renowned political scientist V. O. Key in his 1966 study *The Responsible Electorate*. Key's pioneering work on retrospective voting will conclude this part of our study. It may be argued that historical coincidence elected Van Buren and Bush, but political scientists offer a means to explain their elections based on more than sheer luck.

## CYCLICAL MODELS

Richard Ellis and Aaron Wildavsky, in *Dilemmas of Presidential Leadership: From Washington through Lincoln*, offer three dominant cultural beliefs that have shaped our nation's political landscape. These beliefs are hierarchy, individualism, and egalitarianism. For most of our history, the United States has opposed hierarchies of all kinds. Most presidents in their study attempted to balance individualism and egalitarianism or one of the two with hierarchy. With our focus on Jackson and Van Buren, we find in Andrew Jackson an archenemy of hierarchies and positions of power. Jackson's era was viewed as one for the common man, a period where the individual could make himself into a self-made man. Jackson spent his two terms attacking leaders and institutions. He first attacked the caucus system and the method of electing presidents, which denied him the prize in 1824. He then moved to attack the powerful Second Bank of the United States and the financial structures he believed gave an unfair advantage to some Americans.

When Jackson's second term was coming to an end, the Whig party failed to offer an alternative leadership style. Jackson viewed himself as the servant of the people and their only national representative. The Whigs proposed a strong government hierarchy, one in contrast to Jackson's focus on individualism. The Whigs wanted political power to reside in Congress and not in the White House. Congress would be made up of the well-educated elite, which was groomed to serve and rule. A Whig election in 1836 would mean the return of the National Bank and many structures Jackson had helped to destroy. Van Buren was viewed as the man to continue protecting the common man from hierarchies and to set the balance between individualism and egalitarianism. The Loco Focos attempted to move the Democratic party to more egalitarian concerns without success. Van Buren faced problems as president when the economy went sour and he would have no one to blame. Jackson had destroyed the financial powers that could have been blamed earlier for economic hardships, but this is beyond our focus. Simply put, in 1836, the Whig alternative vision of hierarchy without a strong president was no match for the continuation of individualism and egalitarianism espoused by Jackson and his hand-picked successor Martin Van Buren.

Although Ellis and Wildavsky use their study to look at only the first sixteen presidents, I believe that one can use it on Reagan and Bush as well. Ronald Reagan came to the presidency under the same climate that had produced Jimmy Carter in 1976. Americans no longer trusted Washington, and they wanted an outsider to lead, just as in 1828. Reagan diminished the role of government in everyone's life, and he campaigned on the theme that government was the problem. Not all of the changes Reagan wanted happened, but there was the sense of renewed individualism that had made America great in its past. Reagan also brought a renewal of patriotism, which made people feel good and helped in shaping a perception of egalitarianism. No one was better than anyone else. Reagan did not have the same hierarchies to attack as in Jackson's day, but he did have the evil empire, in the form of the Soviet Union, on which to focus America's attention.

When Reagan's time at our nation's helm was at an end, America had to decide which direction it wanted to go. Did it want a bureaucratic governor from Massachusetts who wanted an increased role for the federal government and a movement toward greater egalitarianism at the expense of individualism or a vice president who promised to stay the course and continue to downsize government and to make Americans feel good about themselves? In the end, Americans chose George Bush to maintain the cultural beliefs instilled by Ronald Reagan. Like Van Buren, Bush suffered from policies initiated by his predecessor. Jackson had removed effective brakes on the economy; Reagan ran up a huge national debt. Ultimately, Bush's presidency suffered the same fate as Van Buren's. In both instances, the Whigs of 1836 and the Democrats of 1988 failed to offer candidates who would continue the same tenants of leadership style that Americans perceived had helped the country.

In the most recent study of presidential style or leadership, Stephen Skowronek offers four ways to classify presidents and their policies. There are presidents of reconstruction who create a new regime and boldly set up a system that will decay shortly after their terms in office. Other presidents find themselves following politics of disjunction. This type of president has difficulty establishing credibility even for good proposals. These good ideas are usually left for a president of reconstruction to carry out. Another type of president is one who offers politics of articulation. These presidents basically offer the public what they want to hear and promise to continue the policies of the reconstructive president. The final type of president is one who adopts the politics of preemption. These presidents strive to be reconstructive without a clear reason to change the operations of the nation's policies.

Skowronek's study not only provides a clear framework to compare Van Buren and Bush and Jackson and Reagan, but also provides a method to show how similar the predecessors of Reagan and Jackson were as well.

Both John Quincy Adams and Jimmy Carter fit the profile so well that
Skowronek concludes:

The exercise of presidential power today spins out parodies of nineteenth century
prototype. Jimmy Carter, Ronald Reagan, and George Bush did not take the same
test of skill at the bar of the modern presidency, rather, by claiming distinct places
for themselves in an unfolding political drama, they constructed national politics
in ways that bear an eerie, almost surreal, resemblance to that constructed in turn
by John Quincy Adams, Andrew Jackson, and Martin Van Buren.[1]

Van Buren fits into the category of president who follows politics of
articulation. He offered no alternative vision when he ran for president in
1836, and he also had no options when he became president to differ with
Jackson's policies. Old Hickory followed in Jefferson's footsteps and was
America's second reconstructive president. Jackson also succeeded the politics of disjunction followed by John Quincy Adams. The nation was not
ready for the policies of Adams, which included astronomical observatories,
Henry Clay's American System, or efforts to achieve harmony with Central
and South America. Adams was a good man, viewed by many as our nation's greatest secretary of state but not a successful president.

Jackson came to the presidency prepared to repudiate everything Adams
had wanted to do. He voiced many of the same concerns shared by the
average American, and he said that he acted on their behalf. His actions
were popular but not capable of surviving the passage of time. Skowronek
writes: "Moreover, each of these great political leaders—Jefferson, Jackson,
Lincoln, F. D. R. and Reagan—passed on a newly circumscribed regime,
so tenacious as to implicate their successors in another cycle of gradually
accelerating political decay."[2]

In 1836, Van Buren could do nothing else but to campaign on the premise of staying the course. Had the panic of 1837 begun a year earlier, Van
Buren might have been spared his disastrous term as president. Jackson
would have taken the initiative and forced a way out of the panic. One
must not forget, though, the public perception that Van Buren was a close
advisor, if not one of the architects of Jackson's presidency. For Van Buren
not to engage in politics of articulation would have discredited his role in
the Jackson administration. If he had won the presidency anyway, his public perception would have been the purveyor of politics of preemption, and
he probably would have shared the fate of Skowronek's presidents of preemption, John Tyler, Andrew Jackson, and Richard Nixon.

From the perspective of Bush's election, it appears that America was
simply following Skowronek's progression from policies of disjunction, to
politics of reconstruction, and ending with politics of articulation. Jimmy
Carter acted very much like John Quincy Adams when he was president.
The public was not ready to follow Carter, and America seemed to weaken

emotionally during his presidency. Carter also shared similar convictions about the functions of government as John Quincy Adams had articulated in the 1820s. "John Quincy Adams had held out a standard of 'talent and virtue alone.' " Carter asked, "Can our government be competent? Can our government be honest and decent and open?"[3] This theme took hold in a country still reeling from Watergate and Vietnam.

America needed a new beginning, and it got that with Ronald Reagan's election in 1980. Skowronek comments on Reagan: "His most potent political resource was his authority to repudiate. That contingent authority unlocked the charisma of the presidential office, harmonizing its order-shattering, order-affirming, and order-creating impulses. Trumping the authority of the numbers with the disarming entreaties of Andrew Jackson."[4] Like Jackson, Reagan was able to withstand political attack. His teflon image withstood the Iran/Contra debacle. When his term was drawing to a close, America once again needed someone to stay the course. In this instance, it was George Bush, although most Republican candidates in 1988 would not have strayed far from Reagan's mantle.

Bush did not enjoy as great of an advantage as Reagan's vice president as Van Buren had enjoyed under Jackson. As we recall, Bush campaigned directly against Reagan in 1980, and he was viewed as being out of the loop on Iran-Contra, but he did find himself in 1988 as the best candidate capable of following politics of articulation and continuing Reagan's economic policies. Bush unfortunately suffered the same fate as Van Buren by following the often naive economic policies of their predecessors. Skowronek explained Bush's problem, "Drawing out their candidates difference with the tax and spend liberals, Bush's handlers left him hopelessly adrift in the commitments of his predecessor."[5] But in 1988 and 1836, Bush and Van Buren took advantage of what Skowronek called political time to capture the presidency. The political regimes of Jackson and Reagan each lasted eight years and were both beginning to decay, but not before Van Buren and Bush were safely in the White House.

Another political science model, Erwin Hargrove and Michael Nelson's *Presidents, Politics and Policy*, shares many of the ideas espoused by Skowronek and Ellis and Wildavsky. This model concentrates on three types of presidents. The first type is the president of preparation who generates new ideas, but for one reason or another they do not gain acceptance by the public or in Congress. Time is simply not on the side of a president of preparation. A second type of president is classified as a president of achievement. This president gets his initiatives passed however bold and is viewed as a success. "His political situation," Hargrove and Nelson write, "is one of strong but temporary empowerment."[6] The third type of president is one of consolidation. This type of president has the task of maintaining and rationalizing existing programs. These presidents can accomplish great things, but mostly they have caretaker terms in the White House. "There is the added risk of failing to recognize emerging problems," they conclude.[7]

As with Skowronek's work, the presidents who preceded Jackson and Reagan fit into this model's progression. John Quincy Adams was indeed a president of preparation. Many of his ideas were sound, but he happened to be president at the wrong time. The nation wanted a man of bold action, and it elected Andrew Jackson. His presidency was certainly one of achievement. He fundamentally altered the economy and the relationship between the president and Congress as well as his relationship with the people. Jackson's policies caused problems for his successors according to Hargrove and Nelson. "The rush to push presidential programs into law is so great that little time or attention is given to the feasibility of implementing them."[8] Jackson's destruction of the Second Bank of the United States and his specie circular—which required payment in gold and silver for all purchases of government lands issued in 1836—had a considerable impact when the economic panic struck in 1837. When the time came for Jackson to retire, it was natural for the public to turn to a president of consolidation such as Martin Van Buren. Hargrove and Nelson described no period when the nation, after enjoying eight years of a president of achievement, turned to another man to continue initiating new policies. The United States needed a respite. Van Buren promised not to change things during his campaign, while the Whigs campaigned to alter the structures and policies created under Jackson. In the end, the American public decided to continue with Van Buren. Had William Henry Harrison been elected, the Democratic party would have still controlled Congress and probably would have prevented any great initiatives from passing thus making his presidency a stalemate.

Reagan and Bush fit the model as well. During Jimmy Carter's presidency of preparation, with some achievements such as the Camp David Accords, America simply did not respond to him; they wanted a president of action. Reagan's presidency was one of swift action in his first term, where he slashed taxes, increased military spending, and renewed America's almost forgotten pride in itself. Reagan did not enjoy the considerable achievements of Andrew Jackson, but he did change the structure of government and amass a debt that America is still dealing with today. Recall that a president of achievement is known for passing measures without fully realizing their implications. The premise that America's economy would grow at a great enough rate to offset large spending increases may seem foolish today, but in the 1980s, Reagan believed this premise and acted on it.

After eight Reagan years, who would the United States turn to? The choice seemed to be for either a president of preparation or consolidation. The public was relatively happy with Reagan's policies, but Michael Dukakis offered dramatic change. A Dukakis presidency would have resulted in a presidency of preparation or a stalemate. George Bush was the likely alternative. He had questioned Reagan's economic policies in 1980, but by 1988, he was firmly committed to his policies. He faced economic problems, as did Van Buren, and his actions resulted in the loss of support from loyal Reaganites—support that had put him in the White House in the first place.

It seems that the president of consolidation has a very difficult task. Any great action on his or her part antagonizes the supporters of the president of achievement and spells political disaster for the new incumbent. According to Hargrove and Nelson, the only president of consolidation to enjoy a second term was Dwight Eisenhower. Van Buren and Bush were not popular war heroes. They also had to defend the policies of their own party, unlike Eisenhower who had to protect many of the policies created by Roosevelt and Truman. Perhaps being the incumbent vice president was not the only dilemma facing Bush and Van Buren. Another may have been the difficult task of serving in wake of a president of achievement.

The final work examined that uses a cyclical model is James David Barber's *The Pulse of Politics*. Barber argues that presidential elections fall into twelve-year cycles with three phases. The first phase is an election that generates conflict with a clash of competing ideologies. The second phase is an election of conscience that appeals to principle and honesty. The third phase is an election of conciliation in which there is a desire for tranquillity and compromise. Following Barber's progression, the elections of Jackson in 1828 and Reagan in 1980 can be viewed as elections of conflict. After eight years, Van Buren and Bush ran during an election of conciliation and were elected because they were viewed as the best candidates to keep the nation together.

The cyclical theory is very good for showing similarities between Van Buren and Bush, but not for explaining why they were elected president. This model is a better indicator of the type and style of president rather than who the president might be. This concern aside, the previous studies have shown how unique it was for Van Buren and Bush to be elected president. Their time was just right.

## PROSPECTIVE MODELS

The prospective theory is based on the assumption that a voter compares his or her beliefs with the party and its nominee. The voter gives support to the candidate that will pursue future policies based on the statements they have made during the campaign in correlation with the voter's desire. Political scientists have concluded that voters do not act this way. Prospective models are not given much credence in voting studies.

## RETROSPECTIVE MODELS

The final two works move away from political cycle theories expressed in the previous studies. *The Thirteen Keys to the Presidency*, by Allan Lichtman and Ken DeCell, offers a simple formula that removes the focus from personality and leadership style and presents a method to predict who will be the next president. This formula has successfully predicted each presidential election from 1860 to the present. The final theory, established by V. O. Key in *The Responsible Electorate*, does not focus on the candidate, but on the electorate. Both works offer alternative methods to explain why Van Buren and Bush were elected president and why the other incumbent vice presidents in this study—John C. Breckinridge in 1860, Richard Nixon in 1960, and Hubert Humphrey in 1968—were not.

Lichtman and DeCell base their model on two criteria. The first is the performance of the incumbent party in the White House. The second criterion is political trends of the previous four years and the election year itself. "Presidential elections are primarily referenda on the performance—and, to some extent, the luck—of the incumbent administration during the previous four years."[9] Their model does not rely on cycles of political history to explain why someone becomes president. "This approach helps us understand periods of history in their own terms and recognize the commonalities among them. Because the keys are turned according to historical precedent, every new election reanimates the past to disclose the electoral impact—and hence the significance of events in our own time."[10]

The formula for the model is as follows. If the incumbent party has five or less keys turned against it, then the party is reelected. If the party has more than five keys against it, the incumbent party loses the presidency. Here are the thirteen keys this model is based on:

Key  1:  After the midterm elections, the incumbent party holds more seats in the U.S. House of Representatives than it did before the previous election.

Key  2:  There is no serious contest for the incumbent party's nomination.

Key  3:  The incumbent party's candidate is the sitting president.

Key  4:  There is no significant third party or independent campaign.

Key  5:  The economy is not in recession during the election campaign.

Key  6:  Real per capita economic growth during the term equals or exceeds mean growth during the previous two terms.

Key  7:  The incumbent administration effects major changes in national policy.

Key  8:  There is no sustained social unrest during the term.

Key  9:  The incumbent administration is untainted by major scandal.

Key 10:  The incumbent administration suffers no major failure in foreign or military affairs.

Key 11: The incumbent administration achieves a major success in foreign or military affairs.

Key 12: The incumbent party candidate is charismatic or a national hero.

Key 13: The challenging party candidate is not charismatic or a national hero.[11]


Of the thirteen keys, Van Buren only had three keys turned against him. Lichtman and DeCall consider the first four keys as political keys. Key 1 fell for Van Buren because in 1832 the Democratic party gained six seats in the House of Representatives and only lost two seats in the 1834 midterm elections. Key 2 also was in Van Buren's favor, since he gained the Democratic nomination with virtually no opposition. The only political key that went against Van Buren was the third key, since he was not a sitting president. Key 4 remained with Van Buren because the Loco Focos and Anti-Masons failed to organize a significant challenge to Van Buren.

Lichtman and DeCell consider the next seven keys as performance keys, and they are all in Van Buren's favor. The economy in a short-term basis (Key 5) and the long-term economy (Key 6) both remained with the Democrats. Jackson's administration was able to accomplish an economic feat that Americans dream about today. Jackson paid off the national debt in 1835. Debate focused in 1836 on what to do with the revenue surplus. Also, Jackson can be credited with initiating changes in national policy such as the destruction of the Second Bank of the United States and the power and conduct of the presidency. This secured Key 7 for Van Buren.

Jackson's administration also enjoyed relative calm during its eight years. Some problems arose during the nullification crisis of 1832–33. South Carolina had been terribly hurt by high tariffs from 1818 through 1828. John C. Calhoun reasserted the theories of Thomas Jefferson from the 1790s that a state could nullify a federal law that disproportionately harms a state. President Jackson threatened to lead an army into South Carolina, and Calhoun threatened secession. Overall, the unrest was not sustained, and the compromise reached in 1833 brought the crisis to an end, turning Key 8 to Van Buren. Jackson's administration was also free of major scandal. The Eaton Affair occurred, and there was a corrupt toll collector in the customs house in New York City, but neither event showed a pattern of corruption in the Jackson administration, which allowed Van Buren to hang on to Key 9.

Van Buren secured Key 10 because the Jackson presidency did not suffer any foreign policy failure. At one time prior to the settlement of payments with France, there was some rhetoric and a war with France was a possibility, but cooler heads prevailed, preventing any great failure or success. Van Buren lost Key 11, which deals with foreign policy success. Jackson was able to get France to agree to pay spoliation claims from the War of 1812, but this was not a great success.

Lichtman and DeCell consider the final two keys as personality keys.
Van Buren was not charismatic by any means, but a presidential candidate
in 1836 was not expected to speak in public. Van Buren was also not a
national hero as was Andrew Jackson, so he lost Key 12. Van Buren did
maintain Key 13 because his challengers were not charismatic either. William
Henry Harrison was considered by many as a national hero, but in
1836, this was not the focus of the poorly organized Whig campaign. This
situation changed in 1840 when Harrison's exploits were the focus of a
more organized Whig campaign. After using Lichtman and DeCell's model,
Van Buren emerges a victor by losing just three keys.

With the use of the same model, Bush emerges also as a easy victor with
two keys to spare. Key 1 went to Bush because in 1984 the Republicans
gained twelve seats in the House and lost only five in the 1986 midterm
elections. It appeared early in 1988 that Bush would face a prolonged fight
for the Republican nomination. After finishing third in Iowa, it did seem
that the nomination fight would go the distance. Bush recovered quickly to
win the New Hampshire primary and all sixteen primaries and caucuses
on Super Tuesday. The fight for the nomination was over in March and
with that Bush maintained Key 2.

As with Van Buren, Bush lost Key 3 since he was not the incumbent
president. He kept Key 4 since there was no significant independent campaign
in 1988. Bush also enjoyed a strong economy to run on in 1988.
The stock market recovered from its 500-point free fall in October 1987,
and the economy continued to grow throughout the election year. The
Reagan years also produced the longest continued economical growth since
World War II, thus giving Bush both economic keys.

The next several keys also go to Bush. Lichtman and DeCell convincingly
argue that Reagan failed in his second term to produce any major changes
in policy. Reagan had lost control of the Senate and his support in the
House from southern Democrats also dwindled, turning Key 7 against
Bush. Bush maintained Key 8, since there was no sustained social unrest
during the Reagan years. There is a difference of opinion over Key 9, however.
The Reagan administration faced allegations of wrongdoing during
both terms, culminating in the Iran/Contra scandal in 1987. DeCell and
Lichtman give Key 9 to Bush, since these scandals were not the focus of
Dukakis' campaign. I disagree and turn Key 9 against Bush. Iran/Contra
may have not been a big issue for Dukakis, but it was certainly an issue
until Bush secured the Republican nomination. Reporters and Democrats
were waiting throughout the campaign for more damaging evidence about
Bush and Iran/Contra, which would have been used instantly. Dukakis did
frequently discuss competence when attempting to show differences between
himself and Bush. Even with Key 9 turned against him, Bush would
still win the election following this formula.

The Reagan administration did not achieve any great military or foreign success or failure during the second term splitting Keys 10 and 11. Bush did not earn Key 12, although he was a hero during World War II. He also did not have much charisma. The Democrats did not rally behind the charismatic Jesse Jackson or Mario Cuomo. Michael Dukakis was not charismatic either and was not a war hero, giving Key 13 to Bush. Adding up the totals, Bush loses three keys or four keys depending which way one turns Key 9 and wins the election.

An extra benefit of using this model is that it helps to explain why the other incumbent vice presidents failed to capture the presidency. Breckinridge's run for the presidency in 1860 was hampered by seven keys turned against him. Nixon faced nine discrepent keys in his race against Kennedy in 1960. Finally, Hubert Humphrey suffered eight keys against him in his 1968 race against Richard Nixon and George Wallace. More than just attempting to discuss different personalities and relationships, Lichtman and Decell's model enables one to use concrete data to explain why Van Buren and Bush were able to solve the vice presidential dilemma.

The final model is the one developed by V. O. Key. Key's development of the retrospective voting theory was the basis of most of the cyclical models previously discussed. No matter who is running for president, the electorate is primarily concerned with the past performance of the incumbent administration:

The patterns of flow of the major streams of shifting voters graphically reflect the electorate in its great and perhaps principle role as an appraiser of past events, past performances and past actions. It only judges retrospectively; it commands prospectively only insofar as it expresses either approval or disapproval of that which has happened before. Voters may reject what they have known; or they may approve what they have known. They are not likely to be attracted in great numbers by promises of the novel or unknown.[12]

Key developed his model through the extensive use of presidential polling data from the 1930s to his death in the mid-1960s. He concluded that there were three types of voters: switches, standpatters, and new voters. Key was able to explain large shifts in the electorate throughout the 1940s and 1950s. The standpatters remained loyal to their party, but their turnout fluctuated with their interest in the campaign. Getting a majority of the switchers and new voters seemed to be necessary for victory. Key's theory is simple, and it explains why Van Buren and Bush won the presidency and Richard Nixon did not. In the 1960 campaign, Kennedy was able to split the new voters with Nixon and was able to convince a greater percentage of Democrats who had voted for Eisenhower in 1952 and 1956 to return home to the Democratic party.

Van Buren and Bush were able to capitalize on this impulse of the American electorate to judge past performance rather than promises of the future: "The odds are that the electorate as a whole is better able to make a retrospective appraisal of the work of governments than it is to make estimates of the future performance of nonincumbent candidates."[13] Van Buren was able to hold on to most of Jackson's supporters and split the addition of new voters to make it appear that he had more support than Jackson in 1832, while his margin of victory was considerably less. Bush was also able to hold on to most Republican standpatters and split the new voters with Dukakis, while preventing large defections of independent voters with Reagan Democrats to win the presidency. Key's theory of retrospective voting makes it clear that each presidential election is for the incumbent party to lose. The public perceived that Andrew Jackson and Ronald Reagan had done a good job and rewarded both parties by electing Martin Van Buren and George Bush.

# 5

# What About Gore?

With the 2000 presidential election approaching, it appears probable that Al Gore will attempt to become the third sitting vice president to be elected president. How does Gore's experiences fit into this study? Does he share the background and political experience of Van Buren and Bush? Do the political science models described in this study support his election in 2000? Will Gore achieve success or suffer the same fate as Breckinridge, Nixon, and Humphrey?

Albert A. Gore, Jr., was born on March 31, 1948, in Carthage, Tennessee. He shares with George Bush the distinction of being born into a family of wealth and politics. Gore's father Albert, Sr., was a longtime congressman and senator from Tennessee. Gore's father was also a candidate for the Democratic nomination for vice president in 1956, finishing third behind John Kennedy and the eventual nominee Estes Kefauver.

The younger Gore attended the best schools and grew up in the world of Washington politics. A political career seemed likely, if not expected. Geoff Kuhn, a friend of Gore's from St. Albans, an elite prep school, stated: "We all knew he was going to run for President one day, Oh certainly. He has always had a charmed life—or maybe it's karma. His wife, his public life, it's all been perfect. No one who ever knew this guy could even be a bit surprised by this. It would have been outstanding to us if he hadn't run for President sooner or later."[1]

The first big political issue that affected Gore also affected the man for whom he would serve as vice president—Vietnam. Gore opposed the Vietman War as did Bill Clinton, but before Gore could protest, he had to consider his father's political career. By 1970, Gore had graduated from Harvard and had married Mary "Tipper" Aitcheson. His father was out-spoken against the war and was facing a tough reelection fight. Gore de-cided that it would not help his father's campaign if he avoided the draft, so he enlisted. Gore's father lost the election in the fall, and he spent his tour in Vietnam as a journalist.

Gore returned home to become a reporter for a local newspaper. Sud-denly in 1976, Gore decided to run for Congress. He was elected, and after serving eight years in the House, Gore was elected to the Senate in 1984. In 1988, at the age of thirty-nine, Gore decided to run for president. Gore based his campaign on being the candidate of the South and doing well on Super Tuesday primary day. On Super Tuesday, March 8, 1988, Gore won several southern primaries and became a serious contender for the nomi-nation with Jesse Jackson and Michael Dukakis. Gore's campaign floun-dered when it moved north. Gore had been criticized for his unenthusiastic speaking style, which seemed wooden and emotionless. Gore attached his New York campaign to then-Mayor Ed Koch. During the course of the campaign Koch made some disparaging remarks about Jesse Jackson. These statements hurt Gore, and he finished a poor third in the New York pri-mary and quickly dropped out of the race.

Gore did display his future political viability by paying off his campaign debts in just ten weeks. It appeared that 1992 could be Gore's year. Gore faced tragedy, however, in 1989 when his eight-year-old son was hit by a car. Gore spent weeks by his son's bedside, and he reevaluated his political future. In August 1991, Gore announced that he would not seek the Dem-ocratic nomination in 1992.

Many political observers viewed President Bush's reelection in 1992 as a strong possibility. Gore argued that he believed that Bush could be de-feated, but that he did not want to put his family through a grueling cam-paign. Gore concentrated his efforts on his book *Earth in the Balance* and on legislation to protect the environment. His direct involvement in the 1992 election seemed unlikely.

The primary season in 1992 was filled with a collection of candidates willing to take on a very popular George Bush. Paul Tsongas, Tom Harkin, Douglas Wilder, and Bill Clinton did not stir immediate enthusiasm. Bill Clinton emerged, thanks to the media coverage of his personal life, to seize the nomination from Paul Tsongas who lacked the money and the public's imagination. The governor of Arkansas was able to gain the support of the baby boomers and the soccer moms and become a strong opponent of George Bush.

Clinton's choice of Gore as his running mate was somewhat surprising. Gore was from the same region and generation as Clinton. He did offer political experience in Washington that would be beneficial to an outsider like Clinton. Gore also provided, perhaps, a shield for Clinton on Vietnam, since he did serve in that controversial war. Gore followed Clinton on the campaign bus and emphasized that President Bush had lost touch with the economy.

Gore's main contribution to Clinton's campaign was debating the other vice presidential candidates, Dan Quayle and James Stockdale. Gore showed respect for the war hero Stockdale, but then ignored this underwhelming and underprepared choice of third-party candidate Ross Perot. Gore's main opponent was Quayle. Gore took advantage of Quayle's shortcomings and did a good job defending his book from Quayle's attacks. Gore proved that he was more than qualified to be vice president and did give Clinton's campaign a boost.

The Clinton/Gore ticket achieved victory for the baby boomers. The World War II generation had finished its thirty years in power. What would now happen to the newly elected vice president? Gore had stated that he still wanted to be president. "But if somebody had told me in 1988 that come January '93 you'll be inaugurated as Vice President of the United States, I would have said, 'You're nuts.' "[2] As the transition took place, Gore gradually moved into the shadow usually reserved for vice presidents. What has Gore done during his years as vice president?

Gore took a backseat during Clinton's first term. Clinton's wife, Hillary Rodham Clinton enjoyed the spotlight for her efforts to reform health care in America. Gore worked on reinventing government and reducing government spending. Gore's highpoint during the first term was his successful televised debate with Ross Perot on the NAFTA treaty in November 1993.

Gore spent most of this term on the defensive. Questions arose over the president's decisions regarding cabinet members, homosexuals in the military, and the Whitewater land deal. The Democratic Party was stunned in 1994 when it lost control of the House of Representatives for the first time in over forty years. After this disasterous election Clinton and Gore spent the next two years preparing for reelection in 1996.

Gore did a wonderful job fundraising, and the Clinton/Gore team took advantage of the government shutdown in 1995 to gain the upper hand in Newt Gingrich's House and against Republicans looking to replace them in 1996. The Democratic Party ran an effective negative campaign early in 1996 and the Republican Party, led by Robert Dole, never recovered. Gore appeared less stiff and more coherent in his debate with Republican vice-presidential nominee Jack Kemp. In November, Clinton and Gore enjoyed a comfortable victory, but once again they failed to gain 50 percent of the vote.

As the campaign drew to a close, talk of 2000 began. Gore did not want to discuss this issue. "I don't see this as primarily a preparatory job. I'm not focused on making the race myself in the future."[3] President Clinton, looking to his legacy, would probably benefit if Al Gore was elected president in 2000 to carry on his policies and ideas.

During Clinton's second term, Gore concentrated on protecting the environment, but this activity quickly degenerated into a defensive mode. Questions concerning fundraising in 1996 arose and some questions involved Gore. The main problem, however, was with the president and his sex life. The Monica Lewinsky affair would drag on for over a year and led to impeachment proceedings against Clinton.

Clinton survived impeachment, and Gore emerged as the stable family man free from sexual scandal. This could be helpful in 2000. Another emphasis of Clinton's second term has focused on foreign policy. This involved a threat of war between the United States and Saddam Hussein of Iraq, bombing terrorist organizations, and bombing Serbia. Gore was loyal, but military actions tend to place the vice president in the background.

How well will Gore do in 2000? In comparing his years as vice president to those before him who attempted to become president, the results are mixed. Gore shares the benefit of serving a two-term president like Van Buren and Bush. Andrew Jackson and Ronald Reagan, however, were far more popular than Clinton. In both of his elections, Clinton failed to gain a majority of the vote. Gore will not enjoy the feeling that he will be defending the actions of an administration that has not had the support of the public.

Gore shares with Bush the fact that they were not instrumental in getting their predecessors elected. Both Gore and Bush ran for president themselves prior to becoming vice president. Gore, however, did not run directly against Clinton like Bush did against Reagan, but the fact that he has staged a campaign shows that Gore had a constituency before becoming involved with Clinton.

Gore does have the political experience that Van Buren and Bush brought to the table. Politics was the way of life for the Gores. George Bush grew up in this political world as well, and Van Buren was one of the creators of the Democratic Party. All three knew the political system from the grassroots up, which should be an advantage for Gore in 2000. Each failed in their first efforts to either get elected president or to elect someone else. Bush and Van Buren learned their lessons and did not lose again until they attempted to seek reelection to the presidency.

Unfortunately, Gore's vice presidency has been dominated by the scandals of the Clinton administration. Gore has been accused of some misconduct; however, the main scandals have not involved him. George Bush faced scandal as well and was able to convince the public that he was not in the loop regarding the Iran/Contra scandal. However, Bush served a far more popular president, and he could not question too strongly the policies that led to the scandal. Bush needed Reagan if he hoped to succeed him.

On the other hand, Gore does not serve a man with the power or popularity of Andrew Jackson and Ronald Reagan. Gore will enjoy the support of President Clinton, but perhaps he might be better off without Clinton's direct involvement. Clinton can continue guiding a vibrant economy and avoiding international disaster, but Gore's future should not be predicated on what Clinton does for him.

This may be a possible pitfall for Gore. The three vice presidents who failed, Breckinridge, Nixon, and Humphrey, each ran campaigns somewhat independent from their chief executives. Breckinridge and Humphrey faced scandal or an unpopular war and had to break away. Nixon served a president free from scandal, but he needed to run independent from Eisenhower to show that he was his own man.

How do the various models discussed earlier predict the future for Gore? These models focus a great deal on what type of president a vice president is serving. The political time may not be right for Gore in 2000. Many advised Breckinridge to wait before making his run for the presidency. Nixon returned after his defeat in 1960 to capture the presidency in 1968. Humphrey recovered from his narrow defeat in 1968 to become a viable presidential candidate until his death. Whatever the models predict for 2000, Al Gore may not be done as a political player.

What are the dominant cultural beliefs of the Clinton presidency? Many supported President Clinton because he had many of the same problems facing the average American. Using the Ellis and Wildavsky model, one could conclude that the Clinton years were dominated by egalitarianism and heirarchy with a diminished role for individualism. The president has attempted to give government a dominant role in solving the nation's problems. This emphasis on egalitarianism may have gotten Clinton reelected, but this cultural belief has not brought long-lasting success.

Whoever succeeds Clinton probably will have to continue the belief in egalitarianism, but must also increase the belief in individualism. Gore grew up in politics and government. It may be difficult for Gore to run a campaign with a diminished role of government. This may open the way for an outsider to gain the presidency. Gore may be viewed as too much of an insider and unable to respond to problems that government is not able to solve.

The Skowronek model dealt with presidential leadership style, with four types of presidents—reconstruction, disjunction, articulation, and preemption. The Clinton presidency can be argued to be one of disjunction. The United States has enjoyed economic success and the lowest unemployment rate in a generation during the Clinton years. Many good ideas or interesting proposals, however, have had difficulty gaining credibility. Something needs to be done about the nation's health care, education, and social security system. The next president will have to propose possible solutions.

A Gore victory in 2000 may come if Gore articulates a reconstructive leadership style. He will have to make tough decisions to get things done. If not, the programs mentioned above may face disaster sometime next century. The next president will have to get some important initiatives passed. Gore has no chance of victory if he presents a leadership style of articulation. Gore is not a great communicator, and he would have a difficult time arguing that all of Clinton's programs and beliefs should continue.

The Hargrove and Nelson model also offers a prediction of what type of president will follow Clinton. This model involves three types of presidents—preparation, achievement, and consolidation. The Clinton presidency can be viewed as one of preparation. President Clinton has offered some far-reaching proposals, which for various reasons have failed to gain the support of Congress.

The successor of Clinton should be a president of achievement. After eight years of turmoil, any candidate without the baggage that Clinton brought to Washington will enjoy a honeymoon period with Congress. Gore has considerable experience working with Congress and, if elected, will be able to get programs passed. Gore will not be elected, however, if he proposes to maintain all of his predecessor's programs.

These models help to explain what type of president will follow Clinton. What about Gore himself? DeCell and Lichtman's system of thirteen keys can predict if Gore will follow Clinton. (See pages 122–123 for a list of these keys.)

Key 1 turns in Gore's favor. After losing the House of Representatives in 1994, the Democratic Party has gained seats in the subsequent elections. This feat gives Gore the advantage.

Key 2 as of this time is undecided. Currently the vice president's only opposition for the Democratic nomination is former Senator Bill Bradley. His challenge could be a serious one and thus turn this key against Gore. But at this moment, one cannot predict the campaign of one who has been accused of being more stiff than Gore.

Key 3 is the first key turned against Gore. The vice president is not the incumbent president. Had Clinton been removed from office or resigned, Gore would have gained this key. Barring some unforeseen event, Gore will not gain the advantage of the incumbency.

Key 4 is also undecided at this time. Ross Perot ran a viable third-party campaign in both 1992 and 1996. No third-party candidate as yet has considered running in 2000. This key must be left unturned.

Key 5 cannot be turned until 2000. The country is enjoying economic success, but a recession is a possibility next year. Many voters look at their wallets before they cast their ballots on election day.

Key 6 turns in Gore's favor. The real per capita economic growth of the Clinton years has surpassed the mean growth of the previous two terms. The Clinton administration has enjoyed economic success and can claim credit. The incumbent party certainly takes the blame if the economy is failing.

Key 7 is a difficult key to judge. Has the Clinton administration effected major changes in national policy? Does balancing the budget and providing the first surplus in a generation count? Perhaps one can argue that politics will never be the same after Clinton's presidency. Is this a change for the good? Turn this key in favor of Gore.

Key 8 turns in Gore's favor as well. There has been no sustained social unrest in the United States during the Clinton years. The nation's involvement in Serbia could have brought unrest if there had been heavy American casualties.

Key 9 certainly turns against Gore. The Clinton years have been full of scandal. Several cabinet members and the president have been involved in scandals and have been forced to resign. Gore was also accused of wrongdoing during his fundraising activities in 1996.

Key 10 is also open to conjecture. Has the Clinton administration suffered any major failure in foreign or military affairs? Troops have been used many times during the eight Clinton years with some loss of life, but it is difficult to say if any policy has been a disaster. This key will probably turn Gore's way in 2000.

Key 11 must be turned against Gore. The Clinton administration has not achieved a major success in military or foreign affairs. Peace initiatives in the Middle East or in Ireland have not brought secure or lasting peace or praise for the United States.

Key 12 must also be turned against Gore. The vice president is not a charismatic speaker or a war hero. Gore has improved his style since 1988, but he will never be a Jesse Jackson or Mario Cuomo.

Key 13 must remain undecided at this time. George W. Bush is the leading Republican candidate as the primaries approach. He is not a war hero or charismatic. Someone else could enter the Republican field who has these qualities and turn this key against Gore.

After finishing this exercise, Gore has turned four keys in his favor. He has four keys turned against him and five keys that are undecided. Remember that if a candidate has more than five keys turned against him or her, the candidate will lose. For Al Gore to win the presidency in 2000, he must avoid two of the five undecided keys.

V. O. Key and other political scientists argue that people vote retrospectively. Are people happy with the eight years they have lived with Bill Clinton? Do they want someone to carry on his policies? Do they want a president that is untainted by scandal? Al Gore will have to proceed carefully if he wants to follow in the footsteps of Martin Van Buren and George Bush. He will not have a powerful or popular incumbent leading the way. Gore may have to run his campaign away from Clinton and his scandals but yet associate himself with the economic good times. This will be a very difficult path to follow, but it seems necessary for one trying to avoid the vice-presidential dilemma in order to capture the presidency.

# Conclusion

What can a presidential hopeful learn from this comparison of Martin Van Buren and George Bush? Was the vice presidential dilemma a real obstacle to overcome? After this comprehensive study, these questions and many more can be answered. The elections of Martin Van Buren and George Bush were unique historical phenomenons that can only happen in the right circumstances even if they are a century and a half apart.

A presidential hopeful looking at the vice presidency as a possible avenue to the White House must follow, to a certain extent, the paths opened by Van Buren and Bush. Both men had political careers prior to becoming vice president. This experience was useful when they ultimately ran for the presidency. Van Buren, as one of the founders of the Democratic party and architect of Andrew Jackson's 1828 campaign, knew the ins and outs of political organization. When his time came in 1836, Van Buren knew how to organize a national campaign and to not make the mistakes of 1824. In the case of George Bush, his years in the government and as Republican National Committee chairman enabled him to become well acquainted with Republicans from the grass roots up and many of them owed him favors. Bush's loyal service enabled him to gain the trust of Richard Nixon and then Gerald Ford, who placed him in positions that made him a presidential contender.

The vice presidents who failed, John C. Breckinridge, Richard Nixon, and Hubert Humphrey, did not share this background with Van Buren and Bush. When Breckinridge and Nixon ran for the presidency, they were both relatively young men. Their quick rise to the vice presidency prevented them from gaining a grasp for politics at a grass-roots level. Nixon learned this lesson and worked for years to become familiar with Republicans at all levels. Hubert Humphrey had a long career prior to becoming vice president, but he was not an integral part of the political system that nominated him for president. He had been an outsider since his seating at the 1948 Democratic Convention, but twenty years later, Humphrey was caught between the antagonism for the machine-like politics of the Democratic Party and the insiders getting their cues from President Johnson. Reforms would take place after 1968, but they were too late to help Humphrey.

After reaching the vice presidency, an individual must remain loyal and not appear to have any differences with the chief executive. Van Buren and Bush remained blindly loyal even to the extent that some questioned their effectiveness as a future president. Breckinridge, however, was not loyal to President James Buchanan. A good example was Breckinridge's campaign efforts for Stephen Douglas in 1858, which were against the wishes of Buchanan. Nixon remained loyal to President Eisenhower, but he was used as the Republican attack dog. This role was far different than the grandfatherly image projected by Eisenhower. Humphrey's problem with President Johnson was over the issue of Vietnam. As long as he remained committed to Johnson's war policy, Humphrey was hurt in the polls. As soon as Humphrey broke from Johnson, his numbers soared and he nearly pulled off the election. One must remember that Johnson controlled the party machinery, and if Humphrey broke too soon, the president could have made the party nominate someone else.

The question of what type of president a vice president serves under is also a major concern. Jackson and Reagan were action-oriented and immensely popular. Political science models describe them as presidents of achievement and very successful. The country was better off after eight years of these two men in the White House, and it was natural for the public to want more of the same. Breckinridge and Humphrey were not campaigning with popular presidents behind them. James Buchanan has been described as a president of consolidation who acted only to prevent civil war from breaking out while he was in office. Lyndon Johnson had many great achievements, but the Vietnam War had brought his Great Society to a halt. Johnson and Buchanan were also only one-term presidents.

A minor problem arises when looking at Richard Nixon. He served an immensely popular two-term president who could have been elected to a third term if it was constitutional. What hurt Nixon's efforts? Eisenhower has not been viewed as a president of achievement. He was basically a president of consolidation, and after eight years, the public desired some action. Nixon offered change, but in the minds of a slim majority of Americans, John F. Kennedy offered slightly more.

As personal relationships go, a vice president should strive for the closeness enjoyed by Van Buren and Bush. Van Buren enjoyed daily rides with the president and was his handpicked successor. Old Hickory even went on the stump for his chosen successor during an era that did not favor public campaigning. Bush did not enjoy that close of a relationship with Reagan and was not his chosen successor, but after Bush secured the nomination, he could not have asked for a greater effort than Reagan exerted on his behalf during the general election campaign. If Reagan did not respect and genuinely like his vice president after eight years, he could have just gone through the motions of supporting Bush.

Breckinridge rarely spoke with President Buchanan, and they came from different generations. They differed in so many ways that it would have been a shock if Buchanan had campaigned for him. Richard Nixon was also from a different generation than Eisenhower, and they never became close. Eisenhower eventually supported Nixon in 1960 after his efforts for other possible candidates failed. Circumstances, discussed earlier, prevented extensive campaigning by Eisenhower until very late in the race. Advisers to Reagan and Bush pointed out this problem in 1960 and were convinced that Reagan needed to take an active role in the campaign very early on. Hubert Humphrey was basically Lyndon Johnson's whipping boy. He enjoyed no role in the administration and would not have benefited from direct campaigning from the president. Johnson did call for a bombing halt in October and this helped Humphrey, but an earlier settlement might have done the trick for the vice president.

After serving as vice president, one must hope that weak candidates are served up by the opposition party. Van Buren and Bush both enjoyed facing the second tier of opposition candidates. The outcomes may have been different had Henry Clay and Mario Cuomo entered the campaigns. Poor party organization and nationally unknown candidates only help a vice president project a stronger image. The vice presidents who failed either ran in multicandidate fields or faced a far more charismatic opponent than they could contend with.

Breckinridge was not the most popular candidate in his own party in 1860. This distinction fell to Stephen Douglas, but the issue of slavery destroyed the party's unity and brought Breckinridge into the race. With this break, and the remnants of the Whig party running its own candidate, it is not difficult to understand why Abraham Lincoln won in 1860. Richard Nixon had to deal with the charismatic John Kennedy. Although Kennedy was only four years younger, he appeared more youthful and energetic than Nixon. Humphrey faced a similar problem as Breckinridge. He not only had to face a new Nixon, but also George Wallace who would take votes away from Humphrey in the traditional Democratic stronghold of the South.

Even with all of these concerns, a vice president must rely on the public to decide whether they have enjoyed the past administration and would grant the incumbent party another four years. Political scientists argue that retrospective voting was the main factor in the elections of Van Buren and Bush. Had the public not approved of eight years of Reagan and Jackson, they would not have elected men who campaigned to continue where they left off.

The public did not enjoy the four years of the Buchanan administration and wanted a leader of action. Abraham Lincoln was that leader elected in 1860. The public wanted someone like Andrew Jackson who received votes in 1860, fifteen years after his death. The same can be said for Humphrey in 1968. The Vietnam War ruined Johnson's term in office and the public was not ready to award someone the presidency who supported Johnson's war effort. Finally in Nixon's 1960 race, the public wanted some action after eight years of peace and stability with Eisenhower. Richard Nixon was the right man for the wrong time. His time would come eight years later.

If a presidential contender follows the path opened by Van Buren and Bush, perhaps he or she can become the third incumbent vice president to be elected president. Everything, however, must fall right into place. This phenomenon has only happened twice in 150 years. The dilemma solved by Van Buren and Bush was a great accomplishment, and this study supports this conclusion. Van Buren and Bush won the presidency by essentially promising to stay the course. What would happen when the course hit a rough spot? Would the public accept their initiatives or want the policies of Jackson and Reagan to be followed anyway? In solving one dilemma, Van Buren and Bush created another: How to be an effective president after eight years with a president of action and achievement. Success in presidential politics is usually measured by reelection. This possibility was a more daunting task than the original vice-presidential dilemma. Only one president, Thomas Jefferson, successfully served two terms after being the incumbent vice president. The road to the presidency was handled by Van Buren and Bush, but the road to presidential success and reelection is still difficult to achieve.

# Notes

## INTRODUCTION

1. Edgar Waugh, *Second Consul, The Vice Presidency* (Indianapolis: Bobbs-Merrill, 1956), 38.

2. Ibid., 164.

3. Paul F. Boller, Jr., *Presidential Campaigns* (New York: Oxford University Press, 1984), 198.

4. Michael DiSalle, *Second Choice* (New York: Hawthorn Books, 1966), 14.

5. Stephen Ambrose, *Nixon: The Education of a Politician, 1913–1962* (New York: Simon & Schuster, 1987), 559.

6. Carl Solberg, *Hubert Humphrey: A Biography* (New York: W. W. Norton, 1984), 240.

7. Ibid., 322.

8. Ibid., 407.

9. Hubert Humphrey, *The Education of a Public Man: My Life and Politics* (New York: Doubleday & Company, Inc., 1976), 328.

10. Ibid., 367.

11. Ibid., 427.

## 1. BECOMING VICE PRESIDENT

1. Richard Hofstadter, *The Idea of a Party System* (Berkeley: University of California Press, 1969), 224.

2. Josiah Quincy, *Memoir of the Life of John Quincy Adams* (Boston: Phillips, Sampson and Company, 1858), 157.

3. *Albany Argus*, December 28, 1826, 2.

4. *Albany Argus*, September 18, 1828, 2.

5. *Albany Argus*, September 29, 1828, 2.

6. *Albany Argus*, November 4, 1828, 2.

7. *Albany Argus*, December 15, 1828, 2.

8. *Albany Argus*, January 7, 1829, 2–3.

9. *Albany Argus*, March 11, 1829, 2.

10. John C. Fitzpatrick, ed., *The Autobiography of Martin Van Buren* (Washington, D.C.: Government Printing Office, 1920), 224.

11. *Albany Argus*, May 23, 1829, 2.

12. Quincy, 177.

13. Fitzpatrick, 342.

14. *Albany Argus*, April 3, 1830, 2.

15. Fitzpatrick, 373.

16. *Albany Argus*, March 23, 1831, 2.

17. John Spencer Bassett, ed., *Correspondences of Andrew Jackson, Volume IV, 1829–1832* (Washington, D.C.: Carnegie Institute of Washington, 1929), 260.

18. Ibid., 263.

19. *Albany Argus*, May 10, 1831, 2.

20. *Albany Argus*, July 23, 1831, 2.

21. Fitzpatrick, 405.

22. *Albany Argus*, August 12, 1831, 2.

23. Bassett, 385.

24. *Albany Argus*, December 2, 1831, 2.

25. Thomas Hart Benton, *Thirty Years View* (New York: D. Appleton and Company, 1854), 215.

26. Fitzpatrick, 454.

27. Ibid., 503.

28. Benton, 219.

29. William Emmons, *Biography of Martin Van Buren* (Washington, D.C.: Jacob Gideon, Jr., 1835), 144–145.

30. Ibid., 147–148.

31. Bassett, 405.

32. Fitzpatrick, 591.

33. *Albany Argus*, March 5, 1832, 2.

34. Fitzpatrick, 509.

35. Ibid., 225.

36. Ibid., 595.

37. *Albany Argus*, December 8, 1832, 2.

38. *Albany Argus*, March 5, 1832, 2.

39. Doug Weed, *Man of Integrity* (Eugene, Ore.: Harvest House Publishers, 1988), 18.

40. *Washington Post*, January 27, 1980, A6.

41. *Cincinnati Enquirer*, December 18, 1972, 7.

42. Ibid.

43. *Chicago Tribune*, January 20, 1973, 5.

44. *Washington Post*, March 19, 1973, A2.

45. *Washington Post*, September 9, 1973, A11.

46. Nicholas King, *George Bush: A Biography* (New York: Dodd, Mead, 1980), 87.

47. *Washington Post*, August 15, 1974, A28.

48. *Washington Post*, November 10, 1975, A28.

49. *Washington Post*, November 4, 1975, A11.

50. *Washington Post*, November 4, 1975, A15.

51. *Washington Post*, November 27, 1976, A19.

52. *New York Times*, January 6, 1979, A11.

53. *Washington Post*, January 6, 1979, A8.

54. *Washington Post*, January 21, 1979, A12.

55. *New York Times*, January 29, 1979, A13.

56. *Washington Post*, January 27, 1979, A11.

57. *Washington Post*, February 20, 1979, A4.

58. *New York Times*, May 2, 1979, A1.

59. *New York Times*, May 2, 1979, A18.

60. *Washington Post*, May 3, 1979, A19.

61. *Washington Post*, July 22, 1979, D7.

62. *Cincinnati Enquirer*, August 9, 1979, A15.

63. *Washington Post*, September 2, 1979, C7.

64. *Washington Post*, September 6, 1979, A6.

65. *Washington Post*, September 9, 1979, B7.

66. Ibid.

67. *Washington Post*, October 21, 1979, A4.

68. *Washington Post*, November 21, 1979, A17.

69. *Washington Post*, November 25, 1979, C7.

70. Aram Bakshian, *The Candidates 1980* (New Rochelle, N.Y.: Arlington House Publishers, 1980), 199.

71. Ibid.

72. *Washington Post*, January 13, 1980, F5.

73. Ibid.

74. *Washington Post*, February 15, 1980, A15.

75. Jack Germond and Jules Witcover, *Blue Smoke and Mirrors* (New York: Viking, 1981), 117.

76. *Cincinnati Enquirer*, March 5, 1980, 11.

77. *Washington Post*, March 27, 1980, A1.

78. *Washington Post*, April 6, 1980, A19.

79. *Washington Post*, May 22, 1980, A2.

80. *Washington Post*, May 27, 1980, A5.

81. *Washington Post*, May 13, 1980, A4.

82. *Washington Post*, July 14, 1980, A15.

83. *Washington Post*, July 16, 1980, A19.

84. Ibid.

85. *New York Times*, July 18, 1980, A10.

86. *Washington Post*, July 31, 1980, A3.

87. *Washington Post*, September 23, 1980, A3.

88. *Washington Post*, September 7, 1980, A8.

89. Ibid.

90. *Washington Post*, October 22, 1980, A23.

91. *Washington Post*, November 1, 1980, A3.
92. Ibid.
93. *New York Times*, November 5, 1980, A21.
94. *Washington Post*, November 20, 1980, Z16.
95. Ibid.


## 2. AVOIDING THE DILEMMA

1. *Albany Argus*, March 5, 1833, 2.
2. *Albany Argus*, March 12, 1833, 2.
3. *Albany Argus*, April 17, 1833, 2.
4. John Spencer Bassett, ed., *Correspondences of Andrew Jackson, Volume V 1833–1838* (Washington, D.C.: Carnegie Institute of Washington, 1931), 143.
5. Ibid., 212–213.
6. Marquis James, *Andrew Jackson: Portrait of a President* (New York: The Bobbs-Merrill Company, 1937), 337.
7. *Albany Argus*, July 2, 1832, 2.
8. *Albany Argus*, June 19, 1833, 2.
9. *Albany Argus*, July 4, 1833, 2.
10. *Albany Argus*, October 22, 1833, 2.
11. Ibid.
12. *Albany Argus*, October 3, 1834, 4.
13. William Emmons, *Biography of Martin Van Buren* (Washington, D.C.: Jacob Gideon, Jr., 1835), 170–171.
14. *Albany Argus*, March 21, 1835, 2.
15. Bassett, 331.
16. Charles Henry Ambler, *Thomas Ritchie: A Study in Virginia Politics* (Richmond, Va.: Bell Book & Stationery Company, 1913), 170.
17. *Albany Argus*, April 6, 1835, 2.
18. Nicholas King, *George Bush: A Biography* (New York: Dodd, Mead, 1980), 4.
19. Ibid., 146.
20. *Washington Post*, March 22, 1981, A2.
21. Ibid.
22. *Washington Post*, March 30, 1981, A1.
23. Ibid., A8.
24. Ibid.
25. *New York Times*, March 31, 1981, A1.
26. *Washington Post*, April 12, 1981, A9.
27. Ibid., A3.
28. *Washington Post*, December 20, 1981, A14.
29. Ibid., A15.
30. *Washington Post*, February 19, 1982, D2.
31. Ibid.
32. *Washington Post*, April 19, 1982, A5.
33. *Washington Post*, September 19, 1982, A14.
34. Ibid.

35. Ibid.

36. *Washington Post*, October 3, 1982, A1.

37. *Washington Post*, January 11, 1983, A3.

38. *Washington Post*, February 20, 1983, C5.

39. Ibid.

40. *Washington Post*, May 15, 1983, A1.

41. Ibid., A6.

42. Ibid.

43. Ibid., A7.

44. *Washington Post*, October 9, 1983, C7.

45. Walter Shapiro, "At Last—Off and Running," *Newsweek* (February 6, 1984), 14.

46. *Washington Post*, February 18, 1984, A8.

47. *Washington Post*, February 26, 1984, A1.

48. Ibid., A7.

49. *Washington Post*, August 20, 1984, A1.

50. Ibid.

51. *Washington Post*, August 24, 1984, A6.

52. Ibid.

53. Austin Rainey, ed., *The American Elections of 1984* (Washington, D.C.: American Enterprise Institute for Public Policy Research, 1985), 154.

54. Keith Blume, *The Presidential Election Show: Campaign 84 and Beyond on the Nightly News* (South Hadley, Mass.: Bergin & Garvey Publishing, Inc., 1985), 277.

55. Ibid.

56. Rainey, 155.

57. *Washington Post*, October 18, 1984, A21.

58. Blume, 277.

59. *Washington Post*, November 7, 1984, A39.

60. *Washington Post*, November 3, 1984, A6.

61. Rainey, 155.

62. *Washington Post*, November 8, 1984, A51.

63. *Washington Post*, January 11, 1985, A2.

64. Ibid.

65. *Washington Post*, January 21, 1985, G4.

66. Ibid., G5.

67. *Washington Post*, May 24, 1985, A27.

68. Ibid.

69. *Washington Post*, June 26, 1985, A23.

70. *Washington Post*, July 21, 1985, G7.

71. *Washington Post*, December 11, 1985, A23.

72. Ibid.

73. *Washington Post*, December 24, 1985, A24.

74. *Washington Post*, January 24, 1986, A19.

75. Ibid.

76. *Washington Post*, February 25, 1986, A15.

77. *Washington Post*, March 25, 1986, A5.

78. *Washington Post*, June 17, 1986, A23.

79. *Washington Post*, December 3, 1986, A10.
80. *Chicago Tribune*, December 8, 1986, 29.
81. Ibid.
82. *Washington Post*, December 21, 1986, A24.
83. Ibid.
84. *Washington Post*, January 8, 1987, A25.
85. *Washington Post*, February 13, 1987, A27.
86. Ibid.
87. *Washington Post*, March 6, 1987, A16.
88. *Washington Post*, March 20, 1987, A17.
89. Ibid.
90. *Chicago Tribune*, May 7, 1987, 23.
91. Ibid.
92. *Washington Post*, May 27, 1987, A4.
93. James A. Barnes, "Out on His Own," *National Journal* (June 6, 1987), 1452.
94. Ibid., 1453.
95. Ibid., 1456.
96. *Washington Post*, July 5, 1987, A4.
97. *Washington Post*, August 8, 1987, A4.
98. *Washington Post*, August 14, 1987, A6.
99. *USA Today*, September 11, 1987, 11A.
100. Ibid.
101. *New York Times*, October 12, 1987, A33.
102. Ibid.

## 3. SOLVING THE DILEMMA

1. Glyndon Van Deusen, *The Jacksonian Era: 1828–1848* (New York: Harper & Brother, 1959), 98.
2. Charles M. Wiltse, ed., *The Papers of Daniel Webster, Series One Correspondences, Volume Four, 1835–1839* (Hanover, N.H.: University Press of New England, 1980), 48.
3. Ibid., 88–89.
4. Nancy N. Scott, ed., *A Memoir of Hugh Lawson White* (Philadelphia: J. B. Lippincott & Company, 1856), 269.
5. Ibid.
6. Ibid., 331–332.
7. William Henry Harrison Papers (Washington, D.C.: Library of Congress, 1958), 1.
8. David Crockett, *The Life of Martin Van Buren: Heir Apparent to the Government, and the Appointed Successor of General Andrew Jackson* (Philadelphia: Robert Wright, 1835), 4.
9. Ibid., 5–6.
10. Ibid., 13.
11. Ibid., 61.
12. Ibid., 163–164.

13. Ibid., 180.

14. Ibid., 94.

15. Ibid., 20.

16. Steve Tally, *Bland Ambition: From Adams to Quayle—The Cranks, Criminals, Tax Cheats, and Golfers Who Made It to Vice President* (New York: Harcourt Brace Jovanovich, Publishers, 1992), 71.

17. Arthur M. Schlesinger, Jr., *History of American Presidential Elections, Volume One, 1789–1844* (New York: Chelsea House Publishing, 1971), 584.

18. *Albany Argus*, June 1, 1835, 1.

19. Ibid.

20. Robert Seager II, ed., *The Papers of Henry Clay* (Lexington: University Press of Kentucky, 1988), 773.

21. *Albany Argus*, June 15, 1835, 2.

22. Ibid.

23. Seager, 775.

24. *Albany Argus*, July 3, 1835, 2.

25. *Albany Argus*, November 6, 1835, 2.

26. *Albany Argus*, December 10, 1835, 3.

27. *Albany Argus*, November 14, 1835, 2.

28. *Albany Argus*, December 17, 1835, 2.

29. *Albany Argus*, January 19, 1836, 2.

30. *Albany Argus*, February 11, 1836, 2.

31. Robert Meriwether, ed., *Papers of John C. Calhoun* (Columbia: University of South Carolina Press, 1959), 85–86.

32. *Albany Argus*, February 22, 1836, 2.

33. Martin Van Buren, *Opinions of Martin Van Buren, Vice President of the United States, Upon the Powers and Duties of Congress, In Reference to the Abolition of Slavery Either in the Slave Holding States or in the District of Columbia* (Washington, D.C.: Blair & Rives, Printers, 1836), 5.

34. Ibid.

35. Ibid.

36. Ibid., 6.

37. *Albany Argus*, April 6, 1836, 2.

38. Ibid.

39. *Albany Argus*, April 14, 1836, 2.

40. *Albany Argus*, March 30, 1836, 2.

41. Meriwether, 124.

42. *Albany Argus*, May 25, 1836, 2.

43. *Albany Argus*, July 13, 1836, 2.

44. *Albany Argus*, July 1, 1836, 2.

45. *Albany Argus*, July 13, 1836, 2.

46. Scott, 352.

47. *Albany Argus*, August 8, 1836, 2.

48. *Albany Argus*, August 13, 1836, 2.

49. *Albany Argus*, September 14, 1836, 2.

50. John Spencer Bassett, ed., *Correspondences of Andrew Jackson, Volume V, 1833–1838* (Washington, D.C.: Carnegie Institute of Washington, 1931), 428.

51. *Albany Argus*, October 13, 1836, 2.

52. *Albany Argus*, October 18, 1836, 2.

53. *Albany Argus*, November 5, 1836, 2.

54. *Albany Argus*, December 26, 1836, 2.

55. *Albany Argus*, January 25, 1837, 2.

56. *Albany Argus*, February 3, 1837, 2.

57. *Albany Argus*, March 8, 1837, 2.

58. Thomas Hart Benton, *Thirty Years View* (New York: D. Appleton and Company, 1854), 735.

59. *Columbus Dispatch*, October 22, 1987, A9.

60. *Chicago Tribune*, October 29, 1987, 16.

61. Ibid.

62. *Chicago Tribune*, November 1, 1987, C3.

63. Ibid.

64. Doug Weed, *Man of Integrity* (Eugene, Ore.: Harvest House Publishers, 1988), 23.

65. *Los Angeles Times*, November 22, 1987, 1.

66. Ibid., 37.

67. *Washington Post*, December 12, 1987, A26.

68. Antony C. Sutton, *Two Faces of George Bush* (Boring, Ore.: CPA Book Publisher, 1988), 2.

69. Ibid., 63.

70. Ibid., 64.

71. *Washington Post*, January 6, 1988, A6.

72. Richard Cohen, "The Insider Steps Out," *National Journal* (June 27, 1987), 1643.

73. *Washington Post*, January 14, 1988, A7.

74. *Washington Post*, January 20, 1988, A23.

75. *Washington Post*, January 17, 1988, C7.

76. *Washington Post*, January 20, 1988, A23.

77. *New York Times*, January 26, 1988, A19.

78. Ibid.

79. Ibid.

80. *Washington Post*, January 26, 1988, E1.

81. Richard Stengel, "Bushwacked," *Time* (February 8, 1988), 17.

82. Matt Ridley, *Warts and All: The Man Who Would Be Bush* (London: Viking Press, 1989), 47.

83. Jacob V. Lamar, "Dole on a Roll," *Time* (February 22, 1988), 17.

84. *Washington Post*, February 12, 1988, A2.

85. Jacob V. Lamar, "Again the Man to Beat," *Time* (February 29, 1988), 36.

86. *Washington Post*, February 17, 1988, A6.

87. Lamar, 36.

88. *Washington Post*, February 28, 1988, C7.

89. *Washington Post*, March 5, 1988, A12.

90. *Washington Post*, March 8, 1988, A8.

91. Donald Morrison, ed., *The Winning of the White House 1988* (New York: Time, Inc., 1988), 79.

92. *Los Angeles Times*, March 11, 1988, 16.

93. *New York Times*, March 26, 1988, A37.

94. *Washington Post*, March 29, 1988, A17.

95. *Washington Post*, April 11, 1988, A4.

96. Ronald Brownstein, "Running on His Record," *National Journal* (July 18, 1987), 1831.

97. Ibid., 1835.

98. Ibid.

99. *Washington Post*, April 25, 1988, A11.

100. Ibid.

101. Ibid.

102. *Chicago Tribune*, May 12, 1988, 3.

103. *New York Times*, May 13, 1988, D17.

104. Andrew Bilski, "Bush Changes Course," *Maclean's* (May 30, 1988), 34.

105. George Will, "A History Lesson for Woodrow Dukakis," *Newsday* (June 19, 1988), 10.

106. Ibid.

107. *Los Angeles Times*, June 23, 1988, 18.

108. Jack Anderson, "Drug Czar Bush: Many Promises, But Few Results," *Newsday* (June 29, 1988), 72.

109. *Washington Post*, July 3, 1988, C7.

110. Ibid., C2.

111. *Washington Post*, July 8, 1988, A23.

112. Lou Cannon, "Will Reagan Upstage Bush on the Trail?" *Newsday* (July 25, 1988), 48.

113. *Washington Post*, August 13, 1988, A9.

114. Ibid.

115. *Washington Post*, August 15, 1988, A13.

116. Laurance I. Barrett, "The Torch Is Passed," *Time* (August 22, 1988), 16.

117. Ibid., 19.

118. Richard Fly, "A Talk with Bush," *Business Week* (August 22, 1988), 30.

119. Richard Nixon, "All The Pressure Will Be on George Bush," *Newsweek* (August 22, 1988), 29.

120. *Atlanta Constitution*, August 17, 1988, 18.

121. David Broder, *The Man Who Would Be President: Dan Quayle* (New York: Simon & Schuster, 1992), 16.

122. *Atlanta Constitution*, August 19, 1988, 12.

123. Ibid.

124. Ibid.

125. Ibid.

126. *Washington Post*, August 24, 1988, A21.

127. *Los Angeles Times*, September 7, 1988, 7.

128. Ibid.

129. *Washington Post*, September 10, 1988, A1.

130. *Washington Post*, September 15, 1988, A14.

131. *New York Times*, September 26, 1988, A19.

132. *Washington Post*, September 24, 1988, A9.

133. Richard Stengel, "Nine Key Moments," *Time* (November 21, 1988), 56.

134. Howard Fineman, "Why Bush Is Winning," *Newsweek* (October 24, 1988), 18.

135. *Boston Globe*, November 8, 1988, 11.

136. *Los Angeles Times*, November 3, 1988, 15.

137. *Atlanta Constitution*, November 6, 1988, 11.

138. "Dukakis for President," *New Republic* (November 7, 1988), 9.

139. *Atlanta Constitution*, November 8, 1988, 1.

140. *New York Times*, November 9, 1988, A27.

141. *New York Times*, November 10, 1988, B3.

142. *Boston Globe*, November 10, 1988, 17.

143. *Washington Post*, November 10, 1988, A48.

144. Fred Barnes, "Now What," *New Republic* (November 28, 1988), 9.

145. *New York Times*, January 21, 1989, A10.

## 4. EXPLAINING THE VICTORIES

1. Stephen Skowronek, *The Politics Presidents Make: Leadership from John Adams to George Bush* (Cambridge: The Belknap Press of Harvard University Press, 1993), 410.

2. Ibid., 33.

3. Ibid., 62–63.

4. Ibid., 420.

5. Ibid., 437.

6. Erwin C. Hargrove and Michael Nelson, *Presidents, Politics and Policy* (New York: Alfred A. Knopf, 1984), 197.

7. Ibid., 198.

8. Ibid., 264.

9. Ken DeCell and Allan J. Lichtman, *The Thirteen Keys to the Presidency* (Lanham, Md.: Madison Books, 1990), 5.

10. Ibid., 52–53.

11. Ibid., 7.

12. V. O. Key, *The Responsible Electorate* (Cambridge: Harvard University Press, 1966), 61.

13. Ibid., 76.

## 5. WHAT ABOUT GORE?

1. *New York Times*, July 17, 1992, A9.

2. *New York Times*, November 4, 1992, B4.

3. *New York Times*, August 28, 1996, A14.

# Selected Bibliography

## NEWSPAPERS AND MAGAZINES

*Albany Argus*

*Atlanta Constitution*

*Boston Globe*

*Business Week*

*Chicago Tribune*

*Cincinnati Enquirer*

*Columbus Dispatch*

*Dayton Daily News*

*Los Angeles Times*

*Maclean's*

*National Journal*

*New Republic*

*Newsday*

*Newsweek*

*New York Times*

*Time*

*USA Today*

*Washington Post*

## BOOKS, PAPERS, AND DISSERTATIONS

Alexander, Holmes. *The American Talleyrand*. New York: Harper and Row, 1935.

Ambler, Charles Henry. *Thomas Ritchie: A Study in Virginia Politics*. Richmond, Va.: Bell Book & Stationery Company, 1913.

Ambrose, Stephen. *Eisenhower*. New York: Simon & Schuster, 1984.

———. *Nixon: The Education of a Politician, 1913–1962*. New York: Simon & Schuster, 1987.

*The American Heritage Book of Presidents and Famous Americans, Volume Three*. New York: Dell Publishing, 1967.

Anderson, John M., ed. *John C. Calhoun: Basic Documents*. State College, La.: Bald Eagle Press, 1952.

Bakshian, Aram. *The Candidates 1980*. New Rochelle, N.Y.: Arlington House Publishers, 1980.

Barber, James David. *The Pulse of Politics*. New York: W. W. Norton, 1980.

Bartlett, Irving H. *Daniel Webster*. New York: W. W. Norton, 1978.

Bartus, M. R. "The Presidential Election of 1836." Ph.D. diss. Fordham University, 1967.

Bassett, John Spencer, ed. *Correspondences of Andrew Jackson, Volume IV, 1829–1832*. Washington, D.C.: Carnegie Institute of Washington, 1929.

———, ed. *Correspondences of Andrew Jackson, Volume V, 1833–1838*. Washington, D.C.: Carnegie Institute of Washington, 1931.

Beard, Charles A. *The American Party Battle*. New York: The Macmillan Company, 1928.

Benton, Thomas Hart. *Thirty Years View*. New York: D. Appleton and Company, 1854.

Blume, Keith. *The Presidential Election Show: Campaign 84 and Beyond on the Nightly News*. South Hadley, Mass.: Bergin and Garvey Publishing, Inc., 1985.

Blumenthal, Sidney, and Thomas Edsall. *The Reagan Legacy*. New York: Pantheon Books, 1988.

Boller, Paul F., Jr. *Presidential Campaigns*. New York: Oxford University Press, 1984.

Bowers, Claude. *The Party Battles of the Jackson Period*. New York: Houghton & Mifflin Company, 1922.

Broder, David. *The Man Who Would Be President: Dan Quayle*. New York: Simon and Schuster, 1992.

Bush, George. *Looking Forward*. New York: Doubleday, 1987.

Capers, Gerald. *John C. Calhoun, Opportunist, A Reappraisal*. Chicago: Quadrangle Books, 1969.

Chester, Lewis. *An American Melodrama: The Presidential Campaign of 1968*. New York: Viking Press, 1969.

Cleaves, Freeman. *Old Tippecanoe*. New York: Charles Scribner Sons, 1939.

Cole, Donald B. *Martin Van Buren and the American Political System*. Princeton: Princeton University Press, 1984.

Crockett, David. *The Life of Martin Van Buren: Heir Apparent to the Government, and the Appointed Successor of General Andrew Jackson*. Philadephia: Robert Wright, 1835.

Current, Richard N. *Daniel Webster and the Rise of National Conservatism*. Boston: Little, Brown, and Company, 1955.

Davis, William C. *Breckinridge; Statesman, Soldier, Symbol*. Baton Rouge: Louisiana State University Press, 1974.

DeCell, Ken, and Allan J. Lichtman. *The Thirteen Keys to the Presidency*. Lanham, Md.: Madison Books, 1990.

DiSalle, Michael. *Second Choice*. New York: Hawthorn Books, 1966.

Duke, Paul, ed. *Beyond Reagan: Politics of Upheaval*. New York: Warner Books, Inc., 1986.

Duncan, Philip, ed. *Candidates '88*. Washington, D.C.: Congressional Quarterly, Inc., 1988.

Edwards, George C., and Stephen J. Wayne. *Presidential Leadership: Politics and Policy Making*. New York: St. Martin's Press, 1994.

Ellis, Richard, and Aaron Wildavsky. *Dilemmas of Presidential Leadership: From Washington through Lincoln*. New Brunswick, N.J.: Transaction Books, 1989.

Emmons, William. *Authentic Biography of Colonel Richard M. Johnson*. Boston: Published for the proprietor, 1834.

———. *Biography of Martin Van Buren*. Washington, D.C.: Jacob Gideon, Jr., 1835.

Esaray, Logan, ed. *Messages and Letters of William Henry Harrison*. New York: Arno Press, 1975.

Fenno, Richard. *The Making of the Senator: Dan Quayle*. Washington, D.C.: GQ Press, 1989.

Fitzpatrick, John C., ed. *The Autobiography of Martin Van Buren*. Washington, D.C.: Government Printing Office, 1920.

Gammon, Samuel. *The Presidential Campaign of 1832*. New York: Da Capo Press, 1969.

Germond, Jack, and Jules Witcover. *Blue Smoke and Mirrors*. New York: Viking, 1981.

Goebel, Dorothy. *William Henry Harrison: A Political Biography*. Philadelphia: Porcupine Press, 1974.

Goldstein, Joel K. *The Modern Vice Presidency*. Princeton: Princeton University Press, 1982.

Green, James A. *William Henry Harrison: His Life and Times*. Richmond, Va.: Garrett and Massie, Inc., 1941.

Hargrove, Erwin C., and Michael Nelson. *Presidents, Politics and Policy*. New York: Alfred A. Knopf, 1984.

Harwood, Michael. *In the Shadow of Presidents*. Philadelphia: Lippincott, 1966.

Heale, M. J. *The Presidential Quest: Candidates and Images in American Political Culture, 1787–1852*. New York: Longman, Inc., 1982.

Heck, Frank. *Proud Kentuckian*. Lexington: University Press of Kentucky, 1976.

Hilton, Stanley. *Bob Dole: An American Political Phoenix*. Chicago: Contemporary Book, 1988.

Hofstadter, Richard. *The Idea of a Party System*. Berkeley: University of California Press, 1969.

Humphrey, Hubert. *The Education of a Public Man: My Life and Politics*. New York: Doubleday & Company, Inc., 1976.

James, Marquis. *Andrew Jackson; Portrait of a President*. New York: The Bobbs-Merrill Company, 1937.

Kenney, Charles, and Robert Turner. *Dukakis: An American Odyssey*. Boston: Houghton Mifflin Company, 1988.

Key, V. O. *The Responsible Electorate*. Cambridge: Harvard University Press, 1966.

King, Nicholas. *George Bush: A Biography*. New York: Dodd, Mead, 1980.

Light, Paul Charles. *Vice Presidential Power*. Baltimore, Md.: Johns Hopkins University Press, 1984.

Martin Van Buren Papers. Washington, D.C.: Library of Congress, 1962.

McClure, A. K. *Our Presidents and How We Make Them*. New York: Harper & Brothers Publishers, 1900.

McCormick, Richard P. *The Presidential Game: The Origins of American Presidential Politics*. New York: Oxford University Press, 1982.

McIntyre, James, ed. *The Writings and Speeches of Daniel Webster*. Boston: Little, Brown, 1903.

Meriwether, Robert, ed. *Papers of John C. Calhoun*. Columbia: University of South Carolina Press, 1959.

Meyer, Leland. *The Life and Times of Colonel Richard M. Johnson*. New York: Columbia University Press, 1932.

Morrison, Donald, ed. *The Winning of the White House 1988*. New York: Time, Inc., 1988.

Nelson, Michael. *A Heartbeat Away*. New York: Priority Press Publications, 1988.

———. *The Elections of 1988*. Washington, D.C: LQ Press, 1989.

———, ed. *The Presidency and the Political System, Third Edition*. Washington, D.C.: Congressional Quarterly, Inc., 1980.

———, ed. *The Presidency and the Political System, Fourth Edition*. Washington, D.C: Congressional Quarterly, Inc., 1995.

Nixon, Richard. *The Memoirs of Richard Nixon*. New York: Simon & Schuster, Inc., 1990.

Nyhan, David. *The Duke: The Inside Story of a Political Phenomenon*. New York: Warner Books, 1988.

Polsby, Nelson. *The Citizen's Choice: Humphrey or Nixon*. Washington, D.C.: Public Affairs Press, 1968.

Polsby, Nelson, and Aaron Wildavsky. *Presidential Elections: Strategies and Structures of American Politics*. New York: Chatham House Publishers, Inc., 1996.

Quincy, Josiah. *Memoir of the Life of John Quincy Adams*. Boston: Phillips, Sampson and Company, 1858.

Rainey, Austin, ed. *The American Elections of 1980*. Washington, D.C.: American Enterprise Institute for Public Policy Research, 1981.

———, ed. *The American Elections of 1984*. Washington, D.C.: American Enterprise Institute for Public Policy Research, 1985.

Remini, Robert. *Andrew Jackson and the Course of American Democracy, 1833–1845.* New York: Harper & Row, 1984.

———. *Martin Van Buren and the Making of the Democratic Party.* New York: Columbia University Press, 1959.

———. *The Revolutionary Age of Andrew Jackson.* New York: Harper & Row, 1976.

———, ed. *The Papers of Andrew Jackson.* Knoxville: University of Tennessee Press, 1980.

Ridley, Matt. *Warts and All: The Man Who Would Be Bush.* London: Viking Press, 1989.

Schlesinger, Arthur M., Jr. *The Age of Jackson.* Boston: Little, Brown & Company, 1947.

———. *History of American Presidential Elections, Volume One, 1789–1844.* New York: Chelsea House Publishing, 1971.

Scott, Nancy N., ed. *A Memoir of Hugh Lawson White.* Philadelphia: J. B. Lippincott & Company, 1856.

Seager, Robert, II, ed. *The Papers of Henry Clay.* Lexington: University Press of Kentucky, 1988.

Shanks, Henry, ed. *The Papers of William P. Mangum.* Raleigh, N.C.: State Department of Archives and History, 1952.

Skowronek, Stephen. *The Politics Presidents Make: Leadership from John Adams to George Bush.* Cambridge: The Belknap Press of Harvard University Press, 1993.

Solberg, Carl. *Hubert Humphrey: A Biography.* New York: W. W. Norton, 1984.

Southwick, Leslie. *Presidential Also-Rans and Running Mates, 1788–1980.* Jefferson, N.C.: McFarland & Company, 1984.

Stanwood, Edward. *A History of Presidential Elections.* Boston: Houghton, Mifflin & Company, 1888.

Stempel, Guido H., III, and John W. Windhauser. *The Media in the 1984 and 1988 Presidential Campaigns.* Westport, Conn.: Greenwood Press, 1991.

Sutton, Antony C. *Two Faces of George Bush.* Boring, Ore.: CPA Book Publisher, 1988.

Tally, Steve. *Bland Ambition: From Adams to Quayle—The Cranks, Criminals, Tax Cheats, and Golfers Who Made It to Vice President.* New York: Harcourt Brace Jovanovich, Publishers, 1992.

Van Buren, Martin. *Opinions of Martin Van Buren, Vice President of the United States, Upon the Powers and Duties of Congress, In Reference to the Abolition of Slavery Either in the Slave Holding States or in the District of Columbia.* Washington, D.C.: Blair & Rives, Printers, 1836.

Van Deusen, Glyndon. *The Jacksonian Era: 1828–1848.* New York: Harper & Brother, 1959.

Watson, Harry L. *Liberty and Power: The Politics of Jacksonian America.* New York: Hill and Wang, 1990.

Waugh, Edgar. *Second Consul, The Vice Presidency.* Indianapolis: Bobbs-Merrill, 1956.

Wayne, Stephen J. *The Road to the White House 1992.* New York: St. Martin's Press, 1992.

Weed, Doug. *Man of Integrity.* Eugene, Ore.: Harvest House Publishers, 1988.

White, Theodore. *Making of the President 1960*. New York: Atheneum Publishers, 1961.

———. *Making of the President 1968*. New York: Atheneum Publishers, 1969.

William Henry Harrison Papers. Washington, D.C.: Library of Congress, 1958.

Wilson, Clyde N., and Edwin Hemphill, eds. *John C. Calhoun Papers, Volume Ten*. Columbia: University of South Carolina Press, 1959.

Wiltse, Charles M., ed. *The Papers of Daniel Webster: Series One Correspondence, Volume Four, 1835–1839*. Hanover, N.H.: University Press of England, 1980.

Young, Donald. *American Roulette*. New York: Holt, Rinehart & Winston, 1972.

# Index

**About the Author**

VANCE R. KINCADE, JR. teaches American History at Philadelphia University. Professor Kincade specializes in the American presidency.

ISBN 0-275-96866-9

90000>

EAN

9 780275 968663

HARDCOVER BAR CODE